GCSE English

Romeo & Juliet

by William Shakespeare

Romeo and Juliet is a brilliant play, but it's not always easy to understand what's going on. Unless you've got this CGP book, of course...

It contains the full text of all five acts — and we've explained all the difficult parts in modern, day-to-day English. On top of that, we've added helpful notes about the characters, themes, historical background and more.

We've also included plenty of practice questions to test you on what you've learned. Just make sure you've dotted all the 'i's and star-cross'd all the 't's...

The Complete Play

Contents

Introduction to 'Romeo and Juliet' 1
Elizabethan Theatre 2
Stagecraft 3
Performances of 'Romeo and Juliet' 4
Themes and Techniques 5
Characters 6

Act One

Prologue 7
The Chorus summarises the play's action.
Scene 1 7
The Montagues and the Capulets fight. Romeo tells Benvolio he is lovesick.
Scene 2 13
Paris asks Capulet for Juliet's hand in marriage. Romeo finds out that Capulet is hosting a party.
Scene 3 15
Lady Capulet tries to convince Juliet she should marry Paris.
Scene 4 18
Romeo and his friends go to Capulet's party.
Scene 5 21
Romeo and Juliet meet and fall in love.
Practice Questions 25

Act Two

Prologue 26
The Chorus announces that Romeo has fallen in love with Juliet.
Scene 1 26
Romeo climbs into Capulet's orchard. Benvolio and Mercutio try to find him.
Scene 2 28
Juliet appears at her window and talks with Romeo.
Scene 3 33
Romeo asks Friar Lawrence to marry him to Juliet.
Scene 4 35
Romeo tells the Nurse about the wedding arrangements.
Scene 5 40
The Nurse tells Juliet about the wedding arrangements.
Scene 6 42
Romeo and Juliet meet with Friar Lawrence and set off to the church to be married.
Practice Questions 43

Contents

Act Three

Scene 1 44
Tybalt kills Mercutio in a fight. Romeo kills Tybalt in revenge. The Prince banishes Romeo as punishment.

Scene 2 49
The Nurse tells Juliet what has happened.

Scene 3 52
Romeo finds out he has been banished. Friar Lawrence says he will try to help Romeo.

Scene 4 56
Capulet tells Paris that he can marry Juliet.

Scene 5 57
Romeo parts from Juliet having spent the night with her. Capulet tells Juliet that she must marry Paris.

Practice Questions 63

Act Four

Scene 1 64
Friar Lawrence tells Juliet his plan to help her avoid marrying Paris.

Scene 2 67
Capulet moves forward the date of Juliet's wedding to Paris.

Scene 3 68
Juliet drinks Friar Lawrence's potion, which makes her appear as if she is dead.

Scene 4 70
It is the day of the wedding, and the Nurse is sent to fetch Juliet.

Scene 5 71
The Nurse discovers Juliet's body. Everyone believes that Juliet is dead.

Practice Questions 75

Act Five

Scene 1 76
Romeo is told that Juliet is dead. He buys poison so that he can commit suicide.

Scene 2 78
Friar Lawrence finds out that his letter to Romeo, explaining everything, never arrived.

Scene 3 79
Romeo kills Paris and drinks the poison. Juliet kills herself. Friar Lawrence explains everything. The feud ends.

Practice Questions 87

Practice Questions 88
The Characters from 'Romeo and Juliet'
'Romeo and Juliet' Cartoon

Published by CGP

Editors:
David Broadbent
Luke von Kotze
Anthony Muller
Holly Poynton

With thanks to Claire Boulter, Jennifer Underwood and Nicola Woodfin for the proofreading.

Acknowledgements
Images of the Montagues on page 6 from the Shakespeare's Globe Theatre production of Romeo & Juliet, photographer John Haynes
With thanks to Donald Cooper/photostage.co.uk for permission to use the images on pages 1, 18, 24, 27, 32 and 33
With thanks to iStockphoto.com for permission to use the image on page 2
With thanks to Getty Images for permission to use the image on page 2
With thanks to TopFoto.co.uk for permission to use the image on page 21
With thanks to Rex Features for permission to use the images on pages 4, 6 and 26
With thanks to The Moviestore Collection for permission to use the images on pages 3, 6, 20, 28, 40, 42, 49, 64, 67 and 71
With thanks to Alamy for permission to use the images on pages 1, 4, 5, 13, 74 and 76
Image on page 6 © 20TH CENTURY FOX / THE KOBAL COLLECTION / MORTON, MERRICK
Images on pages 7, 43 and 48 © PARAMOUNT / THE KOBAL COLLECTION

ISBN: 978 1 84146 122 9
Printed by Elanders Ltd, Newcastle upon Tyne.
Clipart from Corel®

Based on the classic CGP style created by Richard Parsons.

Introduction to 'Romeo and Juliet'

Romeo and Juliet was written by William Shakespeare

- William Shakespeare was an English playwright.
- He wrote some of the most famous plays in the English language, including comedies (such as *Twelfth Night*), tragedies (such as *Othello* and *Hamlet*) and histories (such as *Richard III*).
- *Romeo and Juliet* is one of Shakespeare's tragedies. It was probably written at some point in the early 1590s and it was first published in 1597.
- The play is about Romeo and Juliet's doomed relationship:

  - Romeo and Juliet belong to rival families. They fall in love and secretly get married.
  - Romeo is banished for killing Juliet's cousin. Juliet's parents arrange for her to marry another man.
  - Juliet takes a potion to fake her death so that she can run away with Romeo.
  - Romeo thinks Juliet really is dead and so kills himself. When Juliet finds out that Romeo is dead, she kills herself as well.

It's a play with a mix of elements

Shakespeare took the plot for *Romeo and Juliet* from an English language version of an old Italian story. Shakespeare changed the story so that the play switched between longer and shorter scenes with different moods and styles.

AN EXCELLENT conceited Tragedie OF Romeo and Iuliet.

As it hath been often (with great applause) plaid publiquely, by the right Honourable the L. of Hunsdon his Seruants.

LONDON, Printed by Iohn Danter. 1597

- **Humour** — The beginning of the play contains a lot of crude jokes and puns. Some characters are only in the play to make the audience laugh.
- **Love Story** — Shakespeare shows the two main characters falling in love at first sight, and they risk everything to be together.
- **Fighting** — The fighting in the play starts off as being exciting and comical, but by the end, many of the characters have died violently.
- **Fate** — We learn at the beginning of the play that fate is against Romeo and Juliet — their tragic deaths are foreshadowed throughout the play. This creates drama and suspense.

Elizabethan Theatre

Theatre was popular in Shakespeare's time

- Shakespeare was the most successful playwright of his era, but there was plenty of demand for new plays from other playwrights such as Christopher Marlowe and Thomas Kyd.
- The first successful theatres in London were built in the 1570s. Plays attracted large crowds, including the most wealthy in society.
- The theatre wasn't just for rich people — Shakespeare's audiences included servants and labourers. The poorer people in the audience stood in front of the stage — if it rained, they got wet.
- There was no electricity, so most plays were put on during the day.
- There wasn't much scenery and sets were basic so they could be adapted easily to show several different plays.

William Shakespeare

Shakespeare staged his plays at the Globe Theatre

Shakespeare's theatre company performed at the Globe Theatre in London. This is what it might have looked like:

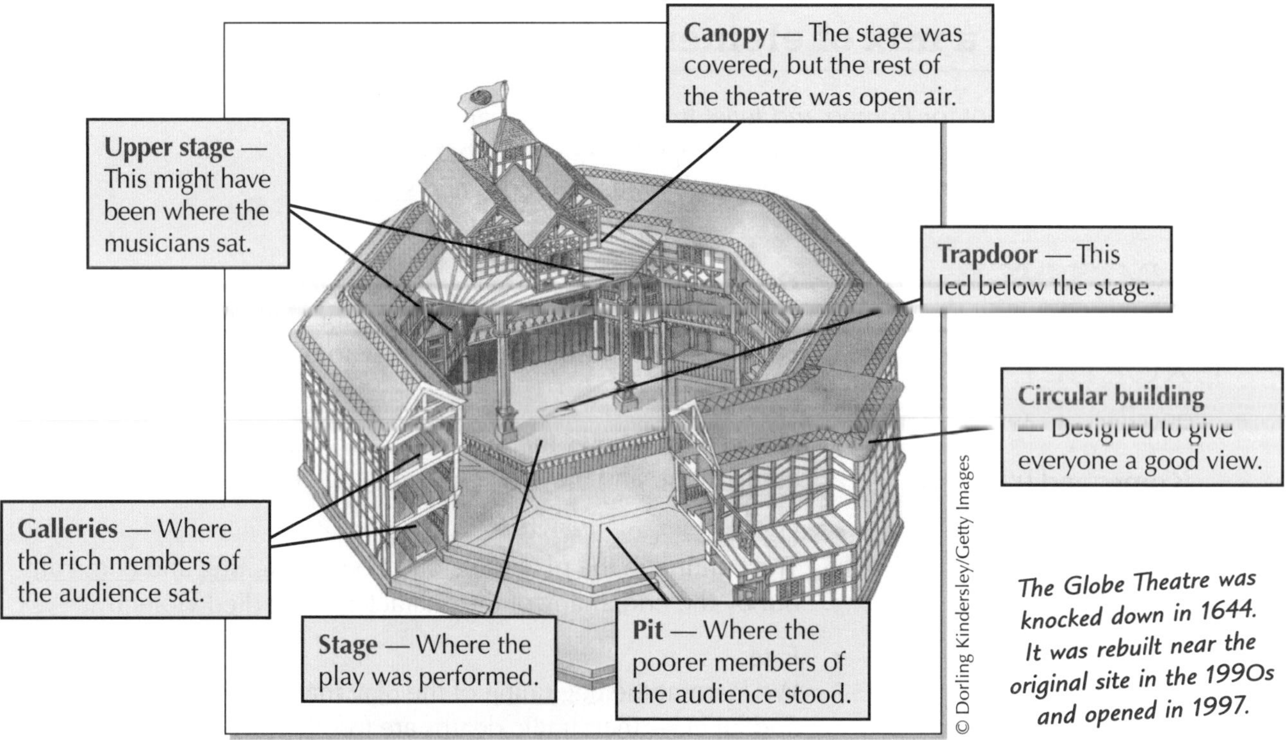
Canopy — The stage was covered, but the rest of the theatre was open air.
Upper stage — This might have been where the musicians sat.
Trapdoor — This led below the stage.
Circular building — Designed to give everyone a good view.
Galleries — Where the rich members of the audience sat.
Stage — Where the play was performed.
Pit — Where the poorer members of the audience stood.

The Globe Theatre was knocked down in 1644. It was rebuilt near the original site in the 1990s and opened in 1997.

Stagecraft

There's more to the play than just the words

Romeo and Juliet is meant to be watched not read — when you read the play, imagine how the action would look on stage. You could think about:

'Stagecraft' is the skill of writing a play so that it works well on stage.

© Moviestore Collection Ltd

Tybalt's black suit in Baz Luhrmann's 'Romeo + Juliet' links him with violence and death.

Stage directions

- In Act 1, Scene 5 the stage directions say that music should be played — this helps to create the party atmosphere of the Capulets' ball.

Props

- Props would have been important to Elizabethan audiences to show what was going on. In Act 5, Scene 3 Romeo enters with a torch and a crowbar. This shows that it's night-time and that he intends to force his way into Juliet's tomb.

Costumes

- Juliet is often dressed in a simple, white dress to highlight her youth and innocence.
- In Baz Luhrmann's *Romeo + Juliet*, the two families are dressed in different clothing to set them apart — the Montagues wear colourful Hawaiian shirts, whereas the Capulets wear black designer suits and expensive jewellery.

Setting

- *Romeo and Juliet* is set in Verona — an Italian city. Italy would have seemed exotic to Elizabethan audiences and would have made the play seem more dramatic (see p.48).
- Franco Zeffirelli's film adaptation (1968) was filmed on location in Italy. The film's authentic setting captures the atmosphere of a busy Italian town.

Stage directions tell the actors what to do

When you're reading the play, look at the stage directions — they're little phrases in italics that tell the actors what to do, when to come in and when to leave the stage.

These are the really common stage directions in Shakespeare:

Enter = when someone comes onto the stage

Exit = when one person leaves the stage

Exeunt = when more than one person leaves

Aside = the character is talking to themselves, not to other characters on the stage

An 'aside' is a great way for characters to reveal their inner thoughts to the audience.

Performances of 'Romeo and Juliet'

Romeo and Juliet was created for an Elizabethan stage

© Geraint Lewis/Rex Features

- In Elizabethan times only men were allowed to act on stage — female roles were usually played by boys.
- Most of the actors would have worn elaborate costumes based on the fashions at that time.
- Musicians were used to create atmosphere and sound effects, such as the music at the Capulet's ball in Act 1, Scene 5 and the wedding preparations in Act 4, Scene 4.

The story of *Romeo and Juliet* has been performed for centuries

The way *Romeo and Juliet* has been performed on stage has changed since Shakespeare's time:

- Women were allowed to perform on stage from 1660. Since then, Juliet and the other female characters have generally been played by women.
- In the 1800s, sets, costumes and props became more elaborate. Many supporting characters' roles were cut down so there was more focus on the lead characters.
- Today, there's a lot of variation in the way that *Romeo and Juliet* is performed. In a 2010 version called *Juliet and her Romeo*, an elderly couple played Romeo and Juliet, with the play set in a nursing home.

There have been loads of adaptations

Romeo and Juliet has been made into ballets, operas, musicals and even cartoons. It's one of the most well-known stories in the world.

- Bernstein's musical *West Side Story* (1957) is based on *Romeo and Juliet*. It's set in New York and revolves around two rival street gangs.
- Franco Zeffirelli was one of the first directors to cast young actors in the title roles. Olivia Hussey was 15 when she played Juliet and Leonard Whiting was 17 when he played Romeo in *Romeo and Juliet* (1968).
- Baz Luhrmann's *Romeo + Juliet* (1996) is a film adaptation set in present-day America, but the characters use Shakespeare's original language.

© AF archive / Alamy

The 1961 film version of 'West Side Story'.

Themes and Techniques

The themes are the main ideas of the play

When you write about *Romeo and Juliet*, you'll often have to comment on the themes. Here are the big ones:

- Love — Romeo and Juliet's passionate love drives the action of the play. This contrasts with Mercutio and the Nurse's sexual view of love.
- Conflict — The feud between the play's families leads to the deaths of the lovers. The tragic ending shows how pointless the rivalry is.
- Family — Family loyalty is important to many of the characters, but Romeo and Juliet become more loyal to each other than to their families.
- Fate and Freewill — The characters blame fate for the bad things that happen, but they make risky and dangerous decisions.

The play's language is important

Look out for these techniques as you read the play:

- Soliloquies — when characters speak to themselves, revealing their thoughts to the audience. Juliet's soliloquy in Act 2, Scene 2 reveals her love for Romeo.
- Puns — when words that sound alike are used to create a humorous double meaning. Mercutio's puns add humour to the comic scenes.
- Imagery — metaphors and similes set the play's mood. Romeo and Juliet's love is often described using images of light and heaven, but also darkness and danger.

- Sonnets — sonnets are poems with fourteen lines and a strict rhyme scheme. Sonnets are associated with love — the first fourteen lines spoken between Romeo and Juliet are a sonnet.

O Romeo, Romeo, wherefore art thou Romeo...

Now that you know about *Romeo and Juliet's* background, it's time to tackle the play itself. Think about themes, characters and language techniques as you read through the play — and look out for Shakespeare's stagecraft too...

Characters

There are two rival families in the play

The Montagues

Lord Montague is Romeo's father.

Married

Lady Montague is Romeo's mother.

Friar Lawrence is a father figure to Romeo.

Mercutio is a close friend of Romeo's.

Romeo is a romantic young man who falls in love with Juliet.

Benvolio is Romeo's cousin and his friend.

The Capulets

Lord Capulet is Juliet's father.

Married

Lady Capulet is Juliet's mother.

The Nurse raised Juliet. They're very close.

Paris gets engaged to Juliet.

Engaged

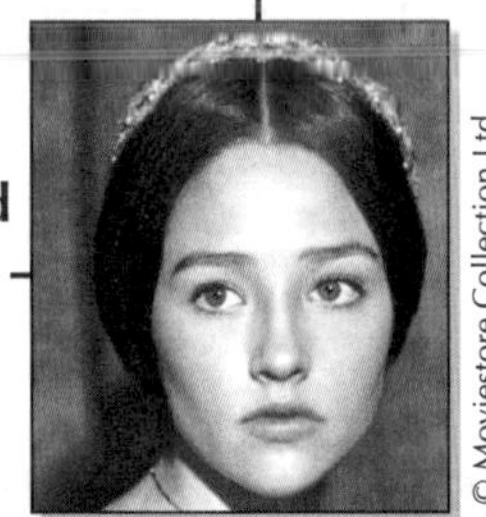

Juliet is a young girl who falls in love with Romeo.

Tybalt is Juliet's cousin.

Act 1, Scene 1 — Romeo is Lovesick

The prologue gives the audience a brief outline of the play. It explains that there is a feud between two families, but from these families come two doomed lovers.

ACT 1, PROLOGUE

Enter CHORUS

CHORUS
Two households, both alike in dignity,
In fair Verona (where we lay our scene),
From ancient grudge break to new mutiny,
Where civil blood makes civil hands unclean.
From forth the fatal loins of these two foes
A pair of star-crossed lovers take their life;
Whose misadventured piteous overthrows
Doth with their death bury their parents' strife.
The fearful passage of their death-marked love,
And the continuance of their parents' rage,
Which, but their children's end, nought could remove,
Is now the two hours' traffic of our stage;
The which if you with patient ears attend,
What here shall miss, our toil shall strive to mend.

Exit

3 'ancient grudge' means 'old feud'.

3 'mutiny' means 'fighting'.

Theme — Fate

Romeo and Juliet are "star-crossed lovers" — we know from the beginning of the play that they're fated to die.

7 'unfortunate downfalls'.

11 In other words, 'Only the death of their children could end the feud.'

There is a sword fight between the Montagues and the Capulets. The Prince of Verona declares that if members of the two families fight again then they will be sentenced to death. Romeo is introduced later in the scene — he's upset because he's in love with Rosaline, who doesn't love him.

ACT 1, SCENE 1

VERONA. A PUBLIC PLACE.

Enter SAMPSON *and* GREGORY, *of the house of Capulet*

SAMPSON Gregory, on my word, we'll not carry coals.
GREGORY No, for then we should be colliers.
SAMPSON I mean, and we be in choler, we'll draw.
GREGORY Ay, while you live, draw your neck out of collar.
SAMPSON I strike quickly, being moved.
GREGORY But thou art not quickly moved to strike.
SAMPSON A dog of the house of Montague moves me.
GREGORY To move is to stir; and to be valiant is to stand: therefore, if thou art moved, thou runn'st away.
SAMPSON A dog of that house shall move me to stand: I will take the wall of any man or maid of Montague's.
GREGORY That shows thee a weak slave, for the weakest goes to the wall.
SAMPSON 'Tis true; and therefore women, being the weaker

1 'carry coals' means 'put up with insults'.

2 a 'collier' is a 'coal miner'.

3 'choler' means 'anger'.

4 'keep your head out of the hangman's noose'.

5 'moved' means 'angered'.

10-11 In other words — 'If I passed a Montague on the street, I would walk closest to the wall to force them into the gutter'.

Act 1, Scene 1

Shakespeare's Techniques

This violent, sexual language contrasts with Romeo and Juliet's tender and gentle love later in the play.

vessels, are ever thrust to the wall: therefore I will push Montague's men from the wall, and thrust his maids to the wall.

GREGORY The quarrel is between our masters and us their men.

SAMPSON 'Tis all one, I will show myself a tyrant: when I have fought with the men, I will be civil with the maids, I will cut off their heads.

GREGORY The heads of the maids?

SAMPSON Ay, the heads of the maids, or their maidenheads; take it in what sense thou wilt.

23 'maidenheads' means 'virginity'.

GREGORY They must take it in sense that feel it.

SAMPSON Me they shall feel while I am able to stand, and 'tis known I am a pretty piece of flesh.

GREGORY 'Tis well thou art not fish; if thou hadst, thou hadst been poor-John. Draw thy tool! Here comes two of the house of Montagues.

29 'poor-John' is a kind of dried fish.

29 'tool' means 'sword'.

Enter ABRAM *and* BALTHASAR

SAMPSON My naked weapon is out. Quarrel, I will back thee.

GREGORY How, turn thy back and run?

SAMPSON Fear me not.

GREGORY No, marry, I fear thee!

SAMPSON Let us take the law of our sides, let them begin.

35 'Let's keep on the right side of the law.'

GREGORY I will frown as I pass by, and let them take it as they list.

36 'list' means 'want'.

SAMPSON Nay, as they dare. I will bite my thumb at them — which is disgrace to them if they bear it.

37 'bite my thumb' — a rude gesture in Shakespeare's day.

ABRAM Do you bite your thumb at us, sir?

SAMPSON I do bite my thumb, sir.

ABRAM Do you bite your thumb at us, sir?

SAMPSON (*Aside to Gregory*) Is the law of our side if I say ay?

GREGORY No.

SAMPSON No, sir, I do not bite my thumb at you, sir, but I bite my thumb, sir.

Theme — Conflict

The conflict between the two families is so deep-rooted that even the servants pick fights with each other.

GREGORY Do you quarrel, sir?

46 'Do you want to start a fight?'

ABRAM Quarrel, sir! No, sir.

SAMPSON If you do, sir, I am for you. I serve as good a man as you.

ABRAM No better.

SAMPSON Well, sir.

Enter BENVOLIO

GREGORY (*Aside to Sampson*) Say 'better', here comes one of my master's kinsmen.

SAMPSON Yes, better, sir.

ABRAM You lie.

SAMPSON Draw, if you be men. Gregory, remember thy washing blow.

56 'washing' means 'slashing'.

They fight

Act 1, Scene 1

BENVOLIO Part, fools!
Put up your swords — you know not what you do.

Beats down their swords

Enter TYBALT

TYBALT What, art thou drawn among these heartless hinds?
Turn thee, Benvolio, look upon thy death.

BENVOLIO I do but keep the peace. Put up thy sword,
Or manage it to part these men with me.

TYBALT What, drawn, and talk of peace! I hate the word,
As I hate hell, all Montagues, and thee:
Have at thee, coward!

They fight

Enter several of both houses, who join the fray.

Then enter three or four CITIZENS *with clubs.*

FIRST CITIZEN Clubs, bills, and partisans! Strike! Beat them down! Down with the Capulets! Down with the Montagues!

Enter CAPULET *in his gown, and* LADY CAPULET

CAPULET What noise is this? Give me my long sword, ho!

LADY CAPULET A crutch, a crutch! Why call you for a sword?

CAPULET My sword, I say! Old Montague is come,
And flourishes his blade in spite of me.

Enter MONTAGUE *and* LADY MONTAGUE

MONTAGUE Thou villain Capulet! Hold me not, let me go.

LADY MONTAGUE Thou shalt not stir one foot to seek a foe.

Enter PRINCE *with Attendants*

PRINCE Rebellious subjects, enemies to peace,
Profaners of this neighbour-stainèd steel —
Will they not hear? What ho! You men, you beasts!
That quench the fire of your pernicious rage
With purple fountains issuing from your veins,
On pain of torture, from those bloody hands
Throw your mistempered weapons to the ground,
And hear the sentence of your movèd prince.
Three civil brawls, bred of an airy word,
By thee, old Capulet, and Montague,
Have thrice disturbed the quiet of our streets,
And made Verona's ancient citizens
Cast by their grave beseeming ornaments
To wield old partisans, in hands as old,
Cankered with peace, to part your cankered hate:
If ever you disturb our streets again,
Your lives shall pay the forfeit of the peace.
For this time all the rest depart away:
You, Capulet, shall go along with me,
And, Montague, come you this afternoon,
To know our further pleasure in this case,
To old Freetown, our common judgement-place.

Character — Benvolio

Benvolio is peaceful — he tries to stop the fight.

59 'Are you fighting with servants?'

Character — Tybalt

Tybalt is a violent character who will fight rather than make peace.

66 'Clubs, bills and partisans' are types of weapon.

71-72 'Montague is waving his sword around to provoke me.'

76 'You who wrongly use your swords on your neighbours.'

78-79 'You put out the fire of your anger with the blood from your wounds.'

87 'grave beseeming ornaments' means 'sober clothes'.

88-89 In other words, 'infected (rusted) weapons have been used to separate the families that have been infected with hate.'

95 'To find out what I wish to do...'

Act 1, Scene 1

Once more, on pain of death, all men depart.

Exeunt all but MONTAGUE, LADY MONTAGUE, *and* BENVOLIO

MONTAGUE Who set this ancient quarrel new abroach?
Speak, nephew, were you by when it began?

BENVOLIO Here were the servants of your adversary,
And yours, close fighting ere I did approach:
I drew to part them — in the instant came
The fiery Tybalt, with his sword prepared,
Which, as he breathed defiance to my ears,
He swung about his head and cut the winds,
Who nothing hurt withal hissed him in scorn:
While we were interchanging thrusts and blows,
Came more and more and fought on part and part,
Till the Prince came, who parted either part.

LADY MONTAGUE O where is Romeo? Saw you him today?
Right glad I am he was not at this fray.

BENVOLIO Madam, an hour before the worshipped sun
Peered forth the golden window of the east,
A troubled mind drive me to walk abroad,
Where underneath the grove of sycamore
That westward rooteth from the city side,
So early walking did I see your son.
Towards him I made, but he was ware of me,
And stole into the covert of the wood:
I, measuring his affections by my own,
Which then most sought where most might not be found,
Being one too many by my weary self,
Pursued my humour, not pursuing his,
And gladly shunned who gladly fled from me.

MONTAGUE Many a morning hath he there been seen,
With tears augmenting the fresh morning's dew.
Adding to clouds more clouds with his deep sighs;
But all so soon as the all-cheering sun
Should in the farthest east begin to draw
The shady curtains from Aurora's bed,
Away from the light steals home my heavy son,
And private in his chamber pens himself,
Shuts up his windows, locks fair daylight out,
And makes himself an artificial night:
Black and portentous must this humour prove,
Unless good counsel may the cause remove.

BENVOLIO My noble uncle, do you know the cause?

MONTAGUE I neither know it, nor can learn of him.

BENVOLIO Have you importuned him by any means?

MONTAGUE Both by myself and many other friends:
But he, his own affections' counsellor,
Is to himself — I will not say how true —
But to himself so secret and so close,
So far from sounding and discovery,
As is the bud bit with an envious worm

98 'Who provoked this old fight again?'

105-106 'He swung his sword around his head, cutting the air, which wasn't hurt and so mocked him by hissing at him.'

111 'Fray' means 'fight'.

118 'ware' means 'aware' or 'wary'.

120-121 'I thought he felt like I did — wanting to be alone'.

123-124 'He wasn't in the mood to talk, and I was happy to leave him alone.'

126 'augmenting' means 'adding to'.

Character — Romeo

This is the first time the audience hears about Romeo. He's portrayed as a wistful and solitary character.

130 'Aurora' is the Roman goddess of the dawn.

131 'heavy' means 'sad'.

135 'portentous' means 'hinting at bad consequences'.

136 'counsel' means 'advice'.

139 'Have you pressed him about it, at all?'

141-142 'He is not open about his feelings — he keeps them to himself.'

Act 1, Scene 1

Ere he can spread his sweet leaves to the air,
Or dedicate his beauty to the sun.
Could we but learn from whence his sorrows grow,
We would as willingly give cure as know.

Enter ROMEO

BENVOLIO See where he comes. So please you, step aside;
I'll know his grievance or be much denied.

MONTAGUE I would thou wert so happy by thy stay,
To hear true shrift. Come, madam, let's away.

Exeunt MONTAGUE *and* LADY MONTAGUE

BENVOLIO Good morrow, cousin.

ROMEO Is the day so young?

BENVOLIO But new struck nine.

ROMEO Ay me! Sad hours seem long.
Was that my father that went hence so fast?

BENVOLIO It was. What sadness lengthens Romeo's hours?

ROMEO Not having that, which, having, makes them short.

BENVOLIO In love?

ROMEO Out —

BENVOLIO Of love?

ROMEO Out of her favour where I am in love.

BENVOLIO Alas that love so gentle in his view,
Should be so tyrannous and rough in proof!

ROMEO Alas, that love, whose view is muffled still,
Should, without eyes, see pathways to his will!
Where shall we dine? O me! What fray was here?
Yet tell me not, for I have heard it all.
Here's much to do with hate, but more with love.
Why, then, O brawling love, O loving hate,
O anything of nothing first create!
O heavy lightness, serious vanity,
Misshapen chaos of well-seeming forms!
Feather of lead, bright smoke, cold fire, sick health!
Still-waking sleep, that is not what it is!
This love feel I, that feel no love in this.
Dost thou not laugh?

BENVOLIO No, coz, I rather weep.

ROMEO Good heart, at what?

BENVOLIO At thy good heart's oppression.

ROMEO Why, such is love's transgression.
Griefs of mine own lie heavy in my breast,
Which thou wilt propagate, to have it pressed
With more of thine; this love that thou hast shown
Doth add more grief to too much of mine own.
Love is a smoke raised with the fume of sighs,
Being purged, a fire sparkling in lovers' eyes,
Being vexed, a sea nourished with lovers' tears:
What is it else? A madness most discreet,

145-146 'He's like a flower bud bitten by a jealous worm before it can open its petals.'

148-149 'If we knew what was wrong, we'd do our best to help him.'

150-151 'Leave it to me — I'll find out what is wrong with him.'

153 'shrift' means 'confession'.

155 'It's just gone nine o'clock.'

156 'hence' means 'from here'.

Theme — Love

When Romeo is in love with Rosaline he's full of self-pity. However, when he's in love with Juliet he's wild and passionate.

163-164 'It's a shame that love, which appears to be so wonderful, can be so harsh in reality.'

165 'sight is blocked (blindfolded)'.

Shakespeare's Techniques

These contradictions suggest that Romeo finds love confusing.

173 'Something ugly created out of a mixture of beautiful things.'

176 'I'm not loved in return.'

179 'transgression' means 'crime'. Romeo is saying that love's crime is to make people sad.

181 'Propagate' means 'make bigger'.

Act 1, Scene 1

187-188 'What else is love? A wise madness, a bitter poison, and a sweet medicine.'

Character — Romeo

This scene shows that Romeo is easily swept up by his emotions.

200 'And the woman I love is beautiful'.

Shakespeare's Techniques

Rosaline has decided to be chaste (pure). This contrasts with Juliet's passionate love for Romeo.

211 'Then she swears she'll stay a virgin?'

213-214 In other words — 'She can't pass on her beauty because she'll never have children.'

217 'She's sworn never to love'.

222 'You should look at other girls.'

222-225 'That will only make me think about how beautiful she is. The masks women wear make us think more about their hidden beauty.'

228-230 In other words — 'Show me someone who is meant to be beautiful, and it'll only remind me of someone more beautiful (Rosaline).'

A choking gall and a preserving sweet.
Farewell, my coz.

BENVOLIO Soft! I will go along;
And if you leave me so, you do me wrong.

ROMEO Tut, I have lost myself; I am not here,
This is not Romeo, he's some other where.

BENVOLIO Tell me in sadness, who is that you love.

ROMEO What, shall I groan and tell thee?

BENVOLIO Groan? Why no,
But sadly tell me, who?

ROMEO Bid a sick man in sadness make his will?
Ah, word ill urged to one that is so ill.
In sadness, cousin, I do love a woman.

BENVOLIO I aimed so near, when I supposed you loved.

ROMEO A right good mark-man! And she's fair I love.

BENVOLIO A right fair mark, fair coz, is soonest hit.

ROMEO Well, in that hit you miss: she'll not be hit
With Cupid's arrow, she hath Dian's wit;
And in strong proof of chastity well armed,
From love's weak childish bow she lives unharmed.
She will not stay the siege of loving terms,
Nor bide th'encounter of assailing eyes,
Nor ope her lap to saint-seducing gold:
O, she is rich in beauty, only poor,
That when she dies with beauty dies her store.

BENVOLIO Then she hath sworn that she will still live chaste?

ROMEO She hath, and in that sparing makes huge waste,
For beauty starved with her severity
Cuts beauty off from all posterity.
She is too fair, too wise, wisely too fair,
To merit bliss by making me despair:
She hath forsworn to love, and in that vow
Do I live dead that live to tell it now.

BENVOLIO Be ruled by me, forget to think of her.

ROMEO O, teach me how I should forget to think.

BENVOLIO By giving liberty unto thine eyes;
Examine other beauties.

ROMEO 'Tis the way
To call hers, exquisite, in question more:
These happy masks that kiss fair ladies' brows,
Being black puts in mind they hide the fair;
He that is strucken blind cannot forget
The precious treasure of his eyesight lost:
Show me a mistress that is passing fair,
What doth her beauty serve, but as a note
Where I may read who passed that passing fair?
Farewell: thou canst not teach me to forget.

BENVOLIO I'll pay that doctrine, or else die in debt.

Exeunt

Act 1, Scene 2 — Capulet Plans a Party

Paris asks for Capulet's permission to marry his daughter, Juliet. Capulet suggests that Juliet is too young to get married, but he invites Paris to his party that evening. Romeo sees that Rosaline is on the guest list and decides to go to the party so that he can see her.

ACT 1, SCENE 2

A STREET

Enter CAPULET, PARIS, *and* SERVANT

CAPULET But Montague is bound as well as I,
In penalty alike, and 'tis not hard, I think,
For men so old as we to keep the peace.

PARIS Of honourable reckoning are you both,
And pity 'tis you lived at odds so long.
But now, my lord, what say you to my suit?

CAPULET But saying o'er what I have said before:
My child is yet a stranger in the world;
She hath not seen the change of fourteen years,
Let two more summers wither in their pride,
Ere we may think her ripe to be a bride.

PARIS Younger than she are happy mothers made.

CAPULET And too soon marred are those so early made.
The earth hath swallowed all my hopes but she,
She is the hopeful lady of my earth.
But woo her, gentle Paris, get her heart,
My will to her consent is but a part;
And she agreed, within her scope of choice
Lies my consent and fair according voice.
This night I hold an old accustomed feast,
Whereto I have invited many a guest,
Such as I love, and you among the store,
One more, most welcome, makes my number more.
At my poor house look to behold this night
Earth-treading stars that make dark heaven light.
Such comfort as do lusty young men feel
When well-apparelled April on the heel
Of limping winter treads, even such delight
Among fresh fennel buds shall you this night
Inherit at my house; hear all, all see,
And like her most whose merit most shall be:
Which on more view, of many, mine being one,
May stand in number, though in reckoning none,
Come, go with me. (*To Servant*) Go, sirrah, trudge about
Through fair Verona; find those persons out
Whose names are written there,

Gives a paper

and to them say,
My house and welcome on their pleasure stay.

1-2 'Montague and I will be punished in the same way if there's another fight.'

8-11 'My daughter is very young, not even fourteen yet — it'll be another two years before she's ready to marry.'

13 'marred' means 'ruined'.

14-17 In other words — 'All my other children have died and she's my only hope for the future. If she falls in love with you then I'll agree to the marriage.'

Theme — Family

Juliet is Capulet's only child, so Capulet has a duty to find her a good match. Paris has very high social status, so their marriage would give Juliet more power and security.

25 'beautiful girls'.

29 'fennel buds' here means 'young women'.

31-33 Something like, 'after seeing all the girls, pick the one you like the best. But to me, no one compares to Juliet.'

34 'sirrah' means 'fellow' — it was used to address boys or people of a lower rank.

37 'They're invited to my house.'

Act 1, Scene 2

39 A 'yard' is a tailor's measuring rod.

40 A 'last' is a shoemaker's tool.

42-44 In other words, 'I can't read. I need to find someone who can.'

47 'holp' means 'helped'.

48-50 In other words, 'Find a new love and the old one will die.'

51 A 'plantain-leaf' is used to bind wounds. Romeo is joking — he thinks that Benvolio's cures are useless for a broken heart.

56 'god-den' means 'good evening'.

62 'You're speaking honestly, have a good day.' — he thinks Romeo is saying that he can't read.

Theme — Fate

Fate plays a role in the tragedy here. The servant can't read, so he asks Romeo to read the invitation. This means that Romeo finds out about the party and so meets Juliet

73 'That's a fine group of people; where are they invited to?'

Exeunt CAPULET *and* PARIS

SERVANT Find them out whose names are written here! It is written that the shoemaker should meddle with his yard, and the tailor with his last, the fisher with his pencil, and the painter with his nets; but I am sent to find those persons whose names are here writ, and can never find what names the writing person hath here writ. I must to the learned. In good time.

Enter BENVOLIO *and* ROMEO

fate because of the story (astrology / horoscope)

BENVOLIO Tut, man, one fire burns out another's burning,
One pain is lessened by another's anguish;
Turn giddy, and be holp by backward turning.
One desperate grief cures with another's languish:
Take thou some new infection to thy eye,
And the rank poison of the old will die.

ROMEO Your plantain-leaf is excellent for that.

BENVOLIO For what, I pray thee?

ROMEO For your broken shin.

BENVOLIO Why, Romeo, art thou mad?

ROMEO Not mad, but bound more than a madman is;
Shut up in prison, kept without my food,
Whipped and tormented and — god-den, good fellow.

SERVANT God gi' god-den. I pray, sir, can you read?

ROMEO Ay, mine own fortune in my misery.

SERVANT Perhaps you have learned it without book: but, I pray, can you read anything you see?

ROMEO Ay, if I know the letters and the language.

SERVANT Ye say honestly, rest you merry.

ROMEO Stay, fellow, I can read.

He reads the letter

'Signior Martino and his wife and daughters,
County Anselme and his beauteous sisters,
The lady widow of Vitruvio,
Signior Placentio and his lovely nieces,
Mercutio and his brother Valentine,
Mine uncle Capulet, his wife and daughters,
My fair niece Rosaline, and Livia,
Signior Valentio and his cousin Tybalt,
Lucio and the lively Helena.'
A fair assembly: whither should they come?

SERVANT Up.

ROMEO Whither?

SERVANT To supper; to our house.

ROMEO Whose house?

SERVANT My master's.

ROMEO Indeed, I should have asked you that before.

SERVANT Now I'll tell you without asking: my master is the great

If Romeo and Juliet meet we get entertained; but we know they will die

Act 1, Scene 3 — Juliet is Not Interested in Marriage

rich Capulet; and if you be not of the house of
Montagues, I pray, come and crush a cup of wine.
Rest you merry!

Exit

BENVOLIO At this same ancient feast of Capulet's
Sups the fair Rosaline whom thou so loves,
With all the admirèd beauties of Verona:
Go thither, and with unattainted eye,
Compare her face with some that I shall show,
And I will make thee think thy swan a crow.

ROMEO When the devout religion of mine eye
Maintains such falsehood, then turn tears to fires;
And these, who often drowned could never die,
Transparent heretics, be burnt for liars!
One fairer than my love! The all-seeing sun
Ne'er saw her match since first the world begun.

BENVOLIO Tut, you saw her fair, none else being by,
Herself poised with herself in either eye;
But in that crystal scales let there be weighed
Your lady's love against some other maid
That I will show you shining at this feast,
And she shall scant show well that now shows best.

ROMEO I'll go along, no such sight to be shown,
But to rejoice in splendour of mine own.

Exeunt

81-82 'and if you're not a Montague, then you're welcome to come and have a drink.'

87 'unattainted eye' means 'an open mind'.

90-93 Something like, 'My eyes are devoted to Rosaline and my tears should burn them if they thought someone else was prettier.'

97 'poised' means 'balanced'.

98 Benvolio advises Romeo to compare Rosaline to other girls. The 'crystal scales' are Romeo's eyes.

102-103 'I'll go to the party, but only to look at Rosaline.'

Lady Capulet tries to persuade Juliet that she's old enough to marry Paris, but Juliet doesn't seem keen to get married. The Nurse spends a lot of the scene telling her favourite story about Juliet as a baby.

ACT 1, SCENE 3

A ROOM IN CAPULET'S HOUSE

Enter LADY CAPULET *and* NURSE

LADY CAPULET Nurse, where's my daughter? Call her forth to me.

NURSE Now, by my maidenhead, at twelve year old,
I bade her come. What, lamb! What, ladybird!
God forbid, where's this girl? What, Juliet!

Enter JULIET

JULIET How now, who calls?

NURSE Your mother.

JULIET Madam, I am here. What is your will?

LADY CAPULET This is the matter. Nurse, give leave awhile,
We must talk in secret. Nurse, come back again,
I have remembered me, thou's hear our counsel.
Thou know'st my daughter's of a pretty age.

NURSE Faith, I can tell her age unto an hour.

Character — The Nurse

The Nurse's first line hints that she lost her virginity at thirteen. This introduces her as a bit crude and tactless.

7 'What can I do for you?'

8 'give leave' means 'leave us'.

10 'you shall hear our conversation.'

Act 1, Scene 3

LADY CAPULET She's not fourteen.
NURSE I'll lay fourteen of my teeth —
And yet, to my teen be it spoken, I have but four —
She is not fourteen. How long is it now
To Lammas-tide?
LADY CAPULET A fortnight and odd days.
NURSE Even or odd, of all days in the year,
Come Lammas-eve at night shall she be fourteen.
Susan and she — God rest all Christian souls! —
Were of an age. Well, Susan is with God,
She was too good for me. But, as I said,
On Lammas-eve at night shall she be fourteen,
That shall she, marry, I remember it well.
'Tis since the earthquake now eleven years,
And she was weaned — I never shall forget it —
Of all the days of the year, upon that day;
For I had then laid wormwood to my dug,
Sitting in the sun under the dove-house wall.
My lord and you were then at Mantua —
Nay, I do bear a brain — but, as I said,
When it did taste the wormwood on the nipple
Of my dug, and felt it bitter, pretty fool,
To see it tetchy and fall out wi'th'dug!
'Shake!' quoth the dove-house; 'twas no need, I trow,
To bid me trudge.
And since that time it is eleven years,
For then she could stand high-lone, nay, by th'rood,
She could have run and waddled all about;
For even the day before, she broke her brow,
And then my husband — God be with his soul,
A'was a merry man — took up the child.
'Yea,' quoth he, 'dost thou fall upon thy face?
Thou wilt fall backward when thou hast more wit;
Wilt thou not, Jule?' and, by my holidame,
The pretty wretch left crying and said, 'Ay.'
To see, now, how a jest shall come about!
I warrant, and I should live a thousand years,
I never should forget it: 'Wilt thou not, Jule?' quoth he,
And, pretty fool, it stinted and said, 'Ay.'
LADY CAPULET Enough of this, I pray thee, hold thy peace.
NURSE Yes, madam, yet I cannot choose but laugh,
To think it should leave crying and say, 'Ay.'
And yet, I warrant, it had upon it brow
A bump as big as a young cockerel's stone,
A perilous knock; and it cried bitterly.
'Yea,' quoth my husband, 'fall'st upon thy face?
Thou wilt fall backward when thou comest to age,
Wilt thou not, Jule?' it stinted and said, 'Ay.'
JULIET And stint thou too, I pray thee, Nurse, say I.
NURSE Peace, I have done. God mark thee to his grace,
Thou wast the prettiest babe that e'er I nursed.

Juliet is a surrogate daughter for the nurse. → nurse is also a surrogate mother to Juliet

13 'lay' means 'bet'.

14 'teen' means 'sadness'.

16 'Lammas-tide' is 1st August.

nurse's daughter

19-20 'She and my daughter Susan were the same age, though Susan's in heaven now.'

nurse speaks lower class english — this implies that she is a comic character.

25 'and I stopped breast-feeding her.'

27 'I put a bitter herb on my breast.'

30 'have a good memory'.

34-35 In other words — 'The dove-house shook (because of the earthquake) and there was no need to tell me to move.'

37 'high-lone' means 'by herself'.

37 'th'rood' means 'Christ's cross'.

39 'She cut her forehead.'

43 'You'll fall backwards' (onto your back for a man).

44 'I swear'.

49 'stinted' means 'stopped'.

Character — Nurse

The nurse tells the same story three times. She's a comedy character, and her humour is often quite daft and vulgar.

51-52 'I can't help laughing when I think about how she stopped crying and said "Yes".'

54 'cockerel's stone' means 'cockerel's testicle'.

55 'perilous knock' means 'a nasty bump'.

joke shows nurse has a light-hearted attitude to sex - deliberate contrast to Romeo and Juliet's attitude to love/sex.

Act 1, Scene 3

And I might live to see thee married once,
I have my wish.

LADY CAPULET Marry, that 'marry' is the very theme
I came to talk of. Tell me, daughter Juliet,
How stands your disposition to be married?

JULIET It is an honour that I dream not of.

NURSE An honour! Were not I thine only nurse,
I would say thou hadst sucked wisdom from thy teat.

LADY CAPULET Well, think of marriage now; younger than you,
Here in Verona, ladies of esteem,
Are made already mothers. By my count,
I was your mother much upon these years
That you are now a maid. Thus then in brief:
The valiant Paris seeks you for his love.

NURSE A man, young lady! Lady, such a man
As all the world — why, he's a man of wax.

LADY CAPULET Verona's summer hath not such a flower.

NURSE Nay, he's a flower, in faith, a very flower.

LADY CAPULET What say you? Can you love the gentleman?
This night you shall behold him at our feast;
Read o'er the volume of young Paris' face,
And find delight writ there with beauty's pen.
Examine every married lineament,
And see how one another lends content
And what obscured in this fair volume lies
Find written in the margent of his eyes.
This precious book of love, this unbound lover,
To beautify him, only lacks a cover.
The fish lives in the sea, and 'tis much pride
For fair without the fair within to hide.
That book in many's eyes doth share the glory,
That in gold clasps locks in the golden story.
So shall you share all that he doth possess,
By having him, making yourself no less.

NURSE No less, nay, bigger. Women grow by men.

LADY CAPULET Speak briefly, can you like of Paris' love?

JULIET I'll look to like, if looking liking move,
But no more deep will I endart mine eye
Than your consent gives strength to make it fly.

Enter SERVANT

SERVANT Madam, the guests are come, supper served up, you called, my young lady asked for, the Nurse cursed in the pantry, and everything in extremity. I must hence to wait, I beseech you, follow straight.

LADY CAPULET We follow thee.

Exit SERVANT

Juliet, the County stays.

NURSE Go, girl, seek happy nights to happy days.

Exeunt

62-63 'I'll be happy if I live to see you married.'

66 'How do you feel about getting married?'

68-69 'If I wasn't the only nurse who breast-fed you, I would say that you had sucked wisdom from the nipple.'

72-75 'By the time I was about your age I'd already given birth to you. To get to the point, Paris wants to marry you.'

77 'He's perfect.'

82-83 'He's very handsome'.

Character — Lady Capulet

Lady Capulet describes Paris in a series of rhyming couplets. This could suggest that she's very excited about the idea of Juliet marrying him.

87 'margent' means 'margin'.

88-89 'When he's bound to you in love, he'll be complete — like a book bound with a cover.'

96 'Men make women pregnant.'

99-100 'endart' means 'throw like a dart'. Juliet is saying something like, 'I'll look, but no more than you would approve of.'

103 'extremity' means 'crisis'.

105 'Juliet, Paris is waiting.' (Paris is a Count.)

Act 1, Scene 4 — Mercutio Talks About Queen Mab

Romeo, Mercutio, Benvolio and their friends are on their way to Capulet's party. Romeo worries about a dream he's had, and Mercutio mocks him for thinking that dreams have any meaning.

ACT 1, SCENE 4

A STREET

Enter ROMEO, MERCUTIO *and* BENVOLIO, *with five or six other Maskers and Torch-bearers*

ROMEO What, shall this speech be spoke for our excuse?
Or shall we on without apology?

BENVOLIO The date is out of such prolixity:
We'll have no Cupid hoodwinked with a scarf,
Bearing a Tartar's painted bow of lath,
Scaring the ladies like a crow-keeper;
Nor no without-book prologue, faintly spoke
After the prompter, for our entrance:
But let them measure us by what they will,
We'll measure them a measure, and be gone.

ROMEO Give me a torch, I am not for this ambling;
Being but heavy, I will bear the light.

MERCUTIO Nay, gentle Romeo, we must have you dance.

ROMEO Not I, believe me. You have dancing shoes
With nimble soles, I have a soul of lead
So stakes me to the ground I cannot move.

MERCUTIO You are a lover; borrow Cupid's wings,
And soar with them above a common bound.

ROMEO I am too sore enpiercèd with his shaft
To soar with his light feathers, and so bound,
I cannot bound a pitch above dull woe:
Under love's heavy burden do I sink.

MERCUTIO And, to sink in it, should you burden love;
Too great oppression for a tender thing.

ROMEO Is love a tender thing? It is too rough,
Too rude, too boisterous, and it pricks like thorn.

MERCUTIO If love be rough with you, be rough with love;
Prick love for pricking, and you beat love down.
Give me a case to put my visage in:
A visor for a visor! What care I
What curious eye doth quote deformities?
Here are the beetle brows shall blush for me.

BENVOLIO Come, knock and enter, and no sooner in,
But every man betake him to his legs.

1-2 Maskers wore masks to parties they weren't invited to. It wasn't considered rude, but they were expected to give a speech.

3 'It's old-fashioned to talk in such a long-winded way (give a speech).'

4 'hoodwinked' means 'blindfolded'.

5 'lath' is cheap wood.

6 'crow-keeper' means 'scarecrow'.

10 'We'll have a dance and then we'll leave.'

Shakespeare's Techniques

Romeo and Mercutio's conversations often have a lot of puns, which makes their relationship seem very close.

15-16 In other words, 'I'm too sad to dance.'

19-20 'I've been hurt by Cupid's arrow too much to be happy and dance.'

23 Something like, 'you'll be a burden on love'.

29 By 'case' he means 'mask'.

29 'visage' means 'face'.

30 'A mask for a mask' — Mercutio could be saying that his face is like a mask.

32 This tells you that Mercutio's mask has thick eyebrows and red cheeks.

Act 1, Scene 4

ROMEO A torch for me: let wantons light of heart
Tickle the senseless rushes with their heels,
For I am proverbed with a grandsire phrase —
I'll be a candle-holder, and look on.
The game was ne'er so fair, and I am done.

MERCUTIO Tut, dun's the mouse, the constable's own word:
If thou art dun, we'll draw thee from the mire
Or — save your reverence — love, wherein thou stickest
Up to the ears. Come, we burn daylight, ho!

ROMEO Nay, that's not so.

MERCUTIO I mean, sir, in delay
We waste our lights in vain, like lamps by day.
Take our good meaning, for our judgement sits
Five times in that ere once in our five wits.

ROMEO And we mean well in going to this mask,
But 'tis no wit to go.

MERCUTIO Why, may one ask?

ROMEO I dreamed a dream tonight.

MERCUTIO And so did I.

ROMEO Well, what was yours?

MERCUTIO That dreamers often lie.

ROMEO In bed asleep, while they do dream things true.

MERCUTIO O, then, I see Queen Mab hath been with you.
She is the fairies' midwife, and she comes
In shape no bigger than an agate-stone
On the forefinger of an alderman,
Drawn with a team of little atomi
Over men's noses as they lie asleep.
Her chariot is an empty hazelnut,
Made by the joiner squirrel or old grub,
Time out a'mind the fairies' coachmakers:
Her wagon-spokes made of long spinners' legs,
The cover of the wings of grasshoppers,
Her traces of the smallest spider web,
Her collars of the moonshine's watery beams,
Her whip of cricket's bone, the lash of film,
Her wagoner a small grey-coated gnat,
Not half so big as a round little worm
Pricked from the lazy finger of a maid.
And in this state she gallops night by night
Through lovers' brains, and then they dream of love;
O'er courtiers' knees, that dream on curtsies straight,
O'er lawyers' fingers, who straight dream on fees,
O'er ladies' lips, who straight on kisses dream,
Which oft the angry Mab with blisters plagues,
Because their breaths with sweetmeats tainted are.
Sometime she gallops o'er a courtier's nose,
And then dreams he of smelling out a suit;
And sometime comes she with a tithe-pig's tail
Tickling a parson's nose as 'a lies asleep,

36 'dance'.

38 'I'll hold a torch and watch everyone else.'

39 'I'm going to quit while the game's good.' — Romeo wants to leave before things go wrong.

41 'If you're unhappy then we'll pull you out, you stick-in-the-mud.'

43-44 'burn daylight' means 'waste time', but Romeo thinks Mercutio means running out of daylight — Romeo's joking because it's already night.

48-49 'We have good intentions going to this party, but it's not a good idea to go.'

Theme — Fate

Romeo's dream fills him with dread — he thinks it is a warning about his fate.

55 'agate-stone' is a small stone used on a ring.

57 'Pulled by a team of tiny beings.'

61 'longer than can be remembered'.

Character — Mercutio

Mercutio's speech about Queen Mab (lines 53-95) is full of playful imagery and puns, which shows that he's intelligent and witty.

64 'traces' means 'harness'.

68-69 It was said that worms came out of the fingers of lazy young women.

71-73 'She makes lovers dream of love, courtiers dream of curtsies, lawyers dream of legal fees...'

Act 1, Scene 4

81 A 'benefice' is an income for a clergyman.

84 'ambuscadoes' means 'ambushes'.

85 'healths' means 'drinks' or 'toasts'.

90 'elflocks' means 'tangled hair'.

92-94 Something like — 'This is the hag who gives sexual dreams to virgins, teaching them how to have sex and bear a child.'

100-103 'Dreams are more changeable than the wind — blowing north then south.'

Shakespeare's Techniques

Shakespeare is hinting at future events here. Romeo's senses that he'll have an 'untimely death'.

112 'He' means 'God' or 'Fate'.

Then dreams he of another benefice.
Sometime she driveth o'er a soldier's neck,
And then dreams he of cutting foreign throats,
Of breaches, ambuscadoes, Spanish blades,
Of healths five-fathom deep; and then anon
Drums in his ear, at which he starts and wakes,
And being thus frighted swears a prayer or two
And sleeps again. This is that very Mab
That plaits the manes of horses in the night,
And bakes the elflocks in foul sluttish hairs,
Which once untangled, much misfortune bodes:
This is the hag, when maids lie on their backs,
That presses them and learns them first to bear,
Making them women of good carriage:
This is she —

ROMEO Peace, peace, Mercutio, peace!
Thou talk'st of nothing.

MERCUTIO True, I talk of dreams,
Which are the children of an idle brain,
Begot of nothing but vain fantasy,
Which is as thin of substance as the air,
And more inconstant than the wind, who woos
Even now the frozen bosom of the north,
And, being angered, puffs away from thence,
Turning his face to the dew-dropping south.

BENVOLIO This wind you talk of blows us from ourselves;
Supper is done, and we shall come too late.

ROMEO I fear too early, for my mind misgives
Some consequence yet hanging in the stars
Shall bitterly begin his fearful date
With this night's revels and expire the term
Of a despisèd life closed in my breast,
By some vile forfeit of untimely death.
But He, that hath the steerage of my course,
Direct my sail! On, lusty gentlemen.

BENVOLIO Strike, drum.

They march about the stage, then stand to one side.

Shakespeare's Techniques

In Act 1, Scene 4, Mercutio mocks people who believe in what they see in their dreams. However, Romeo has two dreams which foreshadow the end of the play.

In Act 1, Scene 4, Romeo talks about a dream which he believes was a warning that there will be bad consequences if he goes to Capulet's ball.

In Act 5, Scene 1, Romeo talks about a dream in which he was dead, but a kiss from Juliet brought him back to life.

Act 1, Scene 5 — Love At First Sight

Romeo and Juliet meet for the first time, at Capulet's party. They fall in love with each other at first sight, but they soon find out that they belong to rival families.

ACT 1, SCENE 5

THE GREAT HALL IN CAPULET'S MANSION

SERVINGMEN *come forth with napkins*

FIRST SERVINGMAN Where's Potpan, that he helps not to take away? He shift a trencher? He scrape a trencher?

SECOND SERVINGMAN When good manners shall lie all in one or two men's hands, and they unwashed too, 'tis a foul thing.

FIRST SERVINGMAN Away with the join-stools, remove the court-cupboard, look to the plate. Good thou, save me a piece of marchpane, and as thou loves me, let the porter let in Susan Grindstone and Nell.

Exit SECOND SERVINGMAN

Anthony and Potpan!

Enter two more SERVINGMEN

THIRD SERVINGMAN Ay, boy, ready.

FIRST SERVINGMAN You are looked for and called for, asked for and sought for, in the great chamber.

FOURTH SERVINGMAN We cannot be here and there too. Cheerly, boys, be brisk a while, and the longer liver take all.

They retire behind

Enter CAPULET, LADY CAPULET, JULIET, TYBALT *and his* PAGE, NURSE, *and all the* GUESTS *and* GENTLEWOMEN *to the Maskers*

CAPULET Welcome, gentlemen! Ladies that have their toes
Unplagued with corns will walk a bout with you.
Ah, my mistresses, which of you all
Will now deny to dance? She that makes dainty,
She I'll swear hath corns. Am I come near ye now?
Welcome, gentlemen! I have seen the day
That I have worn a visor and could tell
A whispering tale in a fair lady's ear,
Such as would please; 'tis gone, 'tis gone, 'tis gone.
You are welcome, gentlemen. Come, musicians, play.

Music plays.

A hall, a hall, give room! And foot it, girls!

And they dance

More light, you knaves, and turn the tables up.
And quench the fire, the room is grown too hot.
Ah, sirrah, this unlooked-for sport comes well.
Nay, sit, nay, sit, good Cousin Capulet,
For you and I are past our dancing days.
How long is't now since last yourself and I
Were in a mask? ← so old he can't remember

the contrast will make Romeo & Juliet seem young and full of life.

COUSIN CAPULET By'r lady, thirty years.

2 'trencher' means 'wooden plate'.

7 'marchpane' means 'marzipan'.

Shakespeare's Techniques

The exit and entrance create a sense of busyness on stage. This emphasises the frantic party atmosphere.

14 'the one who lives the longest takes all' — in other words, you should enjoy life while it lasts.

16 'walk a bout' means 'have a dance'.

18 'acts shyly'.

25 'give room' means 'make room'.

27 'quench' means 'put out'.

Act 1, Scene 5

CAPULET What, man, 'tis not so much, 'tis not so much:
'Tis since the nuptial of Lucentio,
Come Pentecost as quickly as it will,
Some five and twenty years, and then we masked.

COUSIN CAPULET 'Tis more, 'tis more, his son is elder, sir;
His son is thirty.

CAPULET Will you tell me that?
His son was but a ward two years ago.

ROMEO (*To a Servingman*)
What lady's that which doth enrich the hand
Of yonder knight?

SERVINGMAN I know not, sir.

ROMEO O she doth teach the torches to burn bright!
It seems she hangs upon the cheek of night
As a rich jewel in an Ethiop's ear —
Beauty too rich for use, for earth too dear:
So shows a snowy dove trooping with crows,
As yonder lady o'er her fellows shows.
The measure done, I'll watch her place of stand,
And touching hers, make blessèd my rude hand.
Did my heart love till now? Forswear it, sight!
For I ne'er saw true beauty till this night.

TYBALT This, by his voice, should be a Montague.
Fetch me my rapier, boy.

Exit PAGE

What dares the slave
Come hither, covered with an antic face,
To fleer and scorn at our solemnity?
Now by the stock and honour of my kin,
To strike him dead I hold it not a sin.

CAPULET Why, how now, kinsman, wherefore storm you so?

TYBALT Uncle, this is a Montague, our foe:
A villain that is hither come in spite,
To scorn at our solemnity this night.

CAPULET Young Romeo is it?

TYBALT 'Tis he, that villain Romeo.

CAPULET Content thee, gentle coz, let him alone,
'A bears him like a portly gentleman;
And to say truth, Verona brags of him
To be a virtuous and well-governed youth.
I would not for the wealth of all this town
Here in my house do him disparagement;
Therefore be patient, take no note of him;
It is my will, the which if thou respect,
Show a fair presence, and put off these frowns,
An ill-beseeming semblance for a feast.

TYBALT It fits when such a villain is a guest:
I'll not endure him.

CAPULET He shall be endured.

35 'Pentecost' is a Christian festival day.

39 In other words, under 21 years old.

47-48 'She's like a dove among crows.'

Shakespeare's Techniques

This echoes Benvolio in Act 1, Scene 2 (line 89) when he says that Rosaline will seem like a crow when compared with other women.

Theme — Love

Romeo says he's in love with Juliet already, but only three scenes ago he said he loved Rosaline.

54 a 'rapier' is a type of sword.

55 'antic face' means 'horrible mask'.

56 'fleer' means 'mock'.

56 'solemnity' means 'festivities'.

57-58 'By my family's honour I don't think it's wrong to kill him.'

64 'coz' means 'cousin' or 'relative'.

65 'He's acting like a well-mannered person.'

68-69 'I wouldn't do him any harm here in my house for all the money in this town.'

71-73 'Obey my wishes. Look happy and stop frowning — it's the wrong expression for a party.'

Act 1, Scene 5

What, goodman boy, I say he shall, go to!
Am I the master here, or you? Go to!
You'll not endure him? God shall mend my soul,
You'll make a mutiny among my guests!
You will set cock-a-hoop! You'll be the man!

TYBALT Why, uncle, 'tis a shame.

CAPULET Go to, go to,
You are a saucy boy. Is't so indeed?
This trick may chance to scathe you, I know what.
You must contrary me! Marry, 'tis time. —
Well said, my hearts! — You are a princox, go,
Be quiet, or — More light, more light! — For shame,
I'll make you quiet, what! — Cheerly, my hearts!

TYBALT Patience perforce with wilful choler meeting
Makes my flesh tremble in their different greeting:
I will withdraw, but this intrusion shall,
Now seeming sweet, convert to bitterest gall.

Exit

ROMEO (*To Juliet*) If I profane with my unworthiest hand
This holy shrine, the gentle sin is this,
My lips, two blushing pilgrims, ready stand
To smooth that rough touch with a tender kiss.

JULIET Good pilgrim, you do wrong your hand too much,
Which mannerly devotion shows in this,
For saints have hands that pilgrims' hands do touch,
And palm to palm is holy palmers' kiss.

ROMEO Have not saints lips, and holy palmers too?

JULIET Ay, pilgrim, lips that they must use in prayer.

ROMEO O then, dear saint, let lips do what hands do:
They pray — grant thou, lest faith turn to despair.

JULIET Saints do not move, though grant for prayers' sake.

ROMEO Then move not while my prayer's effect I take.
Thus from my lips, by thine, my sin is purged.

Kissing her

JULIET Then have my lips the sin that they have took.

ROMEO Sin from my lips? O trespass sweetly urged!
Give me my sin again.

Kissing her again

JULIET You kiss by th'book.

NURSE Madam, your mother craves a word with you.

ROMEO What is her mother?

NURSE Marry, bachelor,
Her mother is the lady of the house,
And a good lady, and a wise and virtuous.
I nursed her daughter that you talked withal;
I tell you, he that can lay hold of her
Shall have the chinks.

ROMEO Is she a Capulet?

***

80 'You'll cause chaos! You'll be to blame!'

81 'shame' means 'insult'.

82 'saucy' means 'rude'.

85 'princox' means 'insolent boy'.

88-89 'I'm shaking because I'm holding in my anger.'

Shakespeare's Techniques

The first 14 lines spoken between Romeo and Juliet are written as a sonnet — a love poem. It shows that they understand each other straight away.

92-95 Something like — 'If I spoil this shrine (your hand) with my unworthy hand, then my lips are ready to kiss the insult away.'

96-99 'Pilgrim, your touch showed proper devotion — pilgrims touch saints' hands, which is a proper "pilgrim's kiss".'

103 'in case faith turns to despair.'

104 'Saints don't move (because people pray to statues of saints) even when they grant prayers.'

106 'My sin is taken away from my lips by yours.'

107 'Now my lips have got the sin on them.'

109 'as if you'd learnt it from a book' (see the bottom of p.24).

115-116 'Whoever marries her will be rich.'

Act 1, Scene 5

117 'My life is in my enemy's power.'

121 'We're about to have some light refreshments.'

125 'my goodness, it's getting late'.

127 'yond' means 'that'.

134 'I'll die unmarried.'

142 'Anon' means 'right away'.

O dear account! My life is my foe's debt.
BENVOLIO Away, be gone, the sport is at the best.
ROMEO Ay, so I fear, the more is my unrest.
CAPULET Nay, gentlemen, prepare not to be gone,
We have a trifling foolish banquet towards.

They whisper in his ear

Is it e'en so? Why then I thank you all.
I thank you, honest gentlemen, good night.
More torches here! Come on then, let's to bed.
Ah, sirrah, by my fay, it waxes late,
I'll to my rest.

Exeunt all but JULIET *and* NURSE

JULIET Come hither, Nurse. What is yond gentleman?
NURSE The son and heir of old Tiberio.
JULIET What's he that now is going out of door?
NURSE Marry, that I think be young Petruchio.
JULIET What's he that follows here, that would not dance?
NURSE I know not.
JULIET Go ask his name. If he be marrièd,
My grave is like to be my wedding bed.
NURSE His name is Romeo, and a Montague,
The only son of your great enemy.
JULIET My only love sprung from my only hate.
Too early seen unknown, and known too late.
Prodigious birth of love it is to me,
That I must love a loathèd enemy.
NURSE What's this? What's this?
JULIET A rhyme I learnt even now
Of one I danced withal.

One calls within, 'Juliet!'

NURSE Anon, anon!
Come let's away, the strangers all are gone.

Exeunt

Shakespeare's Techniques

Juliet's use of contradictions — "love" / "hate", "early" / "late", "prodigious" (which can mean "monstrous" and "wonderful") — show her confused feelings towards Romeo.

Theme — Conflict

The feud already threatens to ruin Romeo and Juliet's love. They're worried about being loyal to their families.

Character — Juliet

Lines 92-109 show Romeo and Juliet falling in love. Romeo wants to kiss Juliet straight away, but she is more coy — she doesn't encourage Romeo's kisses, but she doesn't discourage them either. She even teases him when she says "you kiss by th'book" — this could mean that Juliet thinks Romeo's kisses are average — as if he's only read about them. But it could also mean that Romeo's kisses are perfect 'textbook' examples.

© Donald Cooper

Act One — Practice Questions

Quick Questions

1) What does the Prince say will be done to any Montagues or Capulets caught fighting?

2) Why is Romeo so sad in Act 1, Scenes 1 and 2?

3) How old is Juliet?

4) Who wants to marry Juliet in Act 1, Scene 2?

5) How does Romeo hear about Capulet's party?

6) Who was the Nurse's daughter and what happened to her?

7) Why does Romeo wear a mask to the Capulets' ball?

8) What has happened to Romeo to make him reluctant to go to the ball?

9) What does Queen Mab do?

10) How does Tybalt recognise Romeo?

In-depth Questions

1) Using Act 1 as a starting point, write down one word for each of the main characters which describes their personality.

2) Why do you think Shakespeare starts by telling the audience how the play is going to end?

3) How do Mercutio and Benvolio feel about Romeo's love for Rosaline?

4) How is Juliet's relationship with the Nurse different from her relationship with her mother?

5) By the end of Act 1, do you think that Romeo is really in love with Juliet? Give reasons for your answer.

6) What do you think of Capulet's character by the end of Act 1?

7) Write an extract from Tybalt's diary describing how he feels about the events of Act 1.

8) Imagine you are a film director. Rewrite the prologue in modern English and make notes about how you would stage it to make it appeal to a modern audience.

Act 2, Scene 1 — Romeo Looks for Juliet

The prologue explains that Romeo has lost interest in Rosaline, and that he's now in love with Juliet.

ACT 2, PROLOGUE

Enter CHORUS

CHORUS
Now old desire doth in his deathbed lie,
And young affection gapes to be his heir —
That fair for which love groaned for and would die,
With tender Juliet matched, is now not fair.
Now Romeo is beloved and loves again,
Alike bewitchèd by the charm of looks,
But to his foe supposed he must complain,
And she steal love's sweet bait from fearful hooks.
Being held a foe, he may not have access
To breathe such vows as lovers use to swear,
And she as much in love, her means much less
To meet her new-belovèd anywhere:
But passion lends them power, time means, to meet
Tempering extremities with extreme sweet.

Exit

2 'gapes' means 'eagerly waits'.

7 'foe supposed' refers to Juliet.

7 'complain' means 'declare his love'.

14 'Balancing danger with sweetness.'

Romeo sneaks into Capulet's garden looking for Juliet.
Mercutio and Benvolio are looking for him, but they soon give up.

ACT 2, SCENE 1

A LANE BY THE WALL OF CAPULET'S ORCHARD

Enter ROMEO

ROMEO
Can I go forward when my heart is here?
Turn back, dull earth, and find thy centre out.

He climbs the wall, and leaps down within it

Enter BENVOLIO *and* MERCUTIO

BENVOLIO
Romeo! My cousin Romeo! Romeo!

MERCUTIO
He is wise,
And on my life hath stol'n him home to bed.

BENVOLIO
He ran this way, and leapt this orchard wall.
Call, good Mercutio.

MERCUTIO
Nay, I'll conjure too.
Romeo! Humours! Madman! Passion! Lover!
Appear thou in the likeness of a sigh,
Speak but one rhyme, and I am satisfied.

2 'I must turn my body back (towards Capulet's mansion) and find Juliet'.

Character — Romeo

Line 7 sums up Romeo's character — he's unpredictable, impulsive and passionate.

7 'humours' means 'moody'.

Act 2, Scene 1

This is supposed to come across funny.

Cry but 'Ay me!' pronounce but 'love' and 'dove',
Speak to my gossip Venus one fair word,
One nickname for her purblind son and heir,
Young Adam Cupid, he that shot so trim,
When King Cophetua loved the beggar-maid!
He heareth not, he stirreth not, he moveth not;
The ape is dead, and I must conjure him.
I conjure thee by Rosaline's bright eyes,
By her high forehead and her scarlet lip,
By her fine foot, straight leg and quivering thigh
And the demesnes that there adjacent lie,
That in thy likeness thou appear to us!

BENVOLIO And if he hear thee, thou wilt anger him.

MERCUTIO This cannot anger him. 'Twould anger him
To raise a spirit in his mistress' circle
Of some strange nature, letting it there stand
Till she had laid it and conjured it down;
That were some spite. My invocation
Is fair and honest, in his mistress' name
I conjure only but to raise up him.

BENVOLIO Come, he hath hid himself among these trees,
To be consorted with the humorous night.
Blind is his love and best befits the dark.

MERCUTIO If love be blind, love cannot hit the mark.
Now will he sit under a medlar tree,
And wish his mistress were that kind of fruit
As maids call medlars, when they laugh alone.
Romeo, that she were, O, that she were
An open-arse, thou a poperin pear!
Romeo, good night: I'll to my truckle-bed.
This field-bed is too cold for me to sleep:
Come, shall we go?

BENVOLIO Go, then; for 'tis in vain
To seek him here that means not to be found.

Exeunt

11 'gossip' means 'old friend'.

12 'purblind' means 'completely blind'.

13 'trim' means 'accurately'.

20 'demesnes' is pronounced 'dimain', and it means 'parkland'.

Theme — Love

Mercutio's sexual puns — 'spirit' (semen or penis), 'circle' (vagina), 'mark' (sex) — focus on the physical side of love to entertain Benvolio, but also to get Romeo to react so that he comes out of hiding.

Performance

Elizabethan plays had simple sets, so Shakespeare uses language to set the scene. Benvolio's description helps the audience to imagine what is going on.

34-38 'medlar', 'open-arse' and 'poperin pear' are all fruits, but are used here as slang terms for genitals.

Mercutio is immature because he can only see womens' bodies, not the person whos body it is.

Puns and Wordplay

Romeo and Juliet is full of puns and wordplay.

- Juliet uses wordplay to hide the true meaning of what she's saying to her mother in Act 3, Scene 5.
- Mercutio's puns mainly make his scenes more humorous, such as his sexual puns in Act 2, Scene 1.
- Mercutio's deliberate twisting of Tybalt's words in Act 3, Scene 1, provokes a deadly fight.

© Donald Cooper

Juliet ends Romeo's 'artificial night' – a new beginning (metaphor)

Act 2, Scene 2 — The Balcony Scene

Romeo overhears Juliet saying she loves him. Romeo reveals himself to Juliet and tells her that he loves her too. They decide to get married.

balcony – she's above like in heaven

© Moviestore Collection Ltd

ACT 2, SCENE 2

balcony shows they are far apart

CAPULET'S ORCHARD

ROMEO *comes forward*

ROMEO
He jests at scars that never felt a wound.
But soft, what light through yonder window breaks?
It is the east, and Juliet is the sun.
Arise, fair sun, and kill the envious moon,
Who is already sick and pale with grief
That thou, her maid, art far more fair than she.
Be not her maid, since she is envious,
Her vestal livery is but sick and green,
And none but fools do wear it; cast it off.

sunrise ← (It is the east…) → the brightest thing – metaphor

JULIET *appears above at a window*

It is my lady, O it is my love!
O that she knew she were!
She speaks, yet she says nothing; what of that?
Her eye discourses, I will answer it.
I am too bold, 'tis not to me she speaks.
Two of the fairest stars in all the heaven,
Having some business, do entreat her eyes
To twinkle in their spheres till they return.
What if her eyes were there, they in her head?
The brightness of her cheek would shame those stars,
As daylight doth a lamp. Her eyes in heaven
Would through the airy region stream so bright
That birds would sing and think it were not night.
See how she leans her cheek upon her hand!
O that I were a glove upon that hand,
That I might touch that cheek!

JULIET
Ay me!

ROMEO (*Aside*)
She speaks.
O speak again, bright angel, for thou art
As glorious to this night, being o'er my head,
As is a wingèd messenger of heaven
Unto the white-upturnèd wondering eyes
Of mortals that fall back to gaze on him,
When he bestrides the lazy-passing clouds,
And sails upon the bosom of the air.

JULIET
O Romeo, Romeo, wherefore art thou Romeo?
Deny thy father and refuse thy name.
Or if thou wilt not, be but sworn my love,

1 'Mercutio jokes because he doesn't know what it's like to be in love'.

8 It was believed that virgins suffered from 'green sickness'.

Theme — Love

Romeo shows that he's still concerned with the sexual side of love, hoping Juliet will give up her virginity.

13 'discourses' means 'talks to me'.

16-17 'ask her eyes to twinkle in their place until they return'.

21 'stream' means 'shine'.

Imagery

Romeo's language is full of religious imagery. This shows how powerful their love is, but also how extreme — they idolise each other.

33 'wherefore art thou' means 'why are you' (a Montague).

Shakespeare's Techniques

Shakespeare uses Juliet's soliloquy to show the audience her true feelings for Romeo.

Act 2, Scene 2

And I'll no longer be a Capulet.

ROMEO (*Aside*) Shall I hear more, or shall I speak at this?

JULIET 'Tis but thy name that is my enemy —
Thou art thyself, though not a Montague.
What's Montague? It is nor hand nor foot,
Nor arm nor face, nor any other part
Belonging to a man. O be some other name!
What's in a name? That which we call a rose
By any other word would smell as sweet;
So Romeo would, were he not Romeo called,
Retain that dear perfection which he owes
Without that title. Romeo, doff thy name,
And for thy name, which is no part of thee,
Take all myself.

ROMEO I take thee at thy word.
Call me but love, and I'll be new baptised;
Henceforth I never will be Romeo.

JULIET What man art thou that thus bescreened in night
So stumblest on my counsel?

ROMEO By a name
I know not how to tell thee who I am.
My name, dear saint, is hateful to myself,
Because it is an enemy to thee;
Had I it written, I would tear the word.

JULIET My ears have yet not drunk a hundred words
Of thy tongue's uttering, yet I know the sound.
Art thou not Romeo, and a Montague?

ROMEO Neither, fair maid, if either thee dislike.

JULIET How camest thou hither, tell me, and wherefore?
The orchard walls are high and hard to climb,
And the place death, considering who thou art,
If any of my kinsmen find thee here.

ROMEO With love's light wings did I o'erperch these walls,
For stony limits cannot hold love out,
And what love can do, that dares love attempt:
Therefore thy kinsmen are no stop to me.

JULIET If they do see thee, they will murder thee.

ROMEO Alack, there lies more peril in thine eye
Than twenty of their swords. Look thou but sweet,
And I am proof against their enmity.

JULIET I would not for the world they saw thee here.

ROMEO I have night's cloak to hide me from their eyes,
And but thou love me, let them find me here.
My life were better ended by their hate,
Than death proroguèd, wanting of thy love.

JULIET By whose direction found'st thou out this place?

ROMEO By Love, that first did prompt me to enquire:
He lent me counsel, and I lent him eyes.
I am no pilot, yet wert thou as far

Theme — Family

Juliet repeats the words 'name', 'Romeo' and 'Montague'. This emphasises how important family relationships are in the play. Juliet knows their family ties will cause them problems.

53 'interrupts my private thoughts'

58-59 'I've barely heard you say anything, but I recognise your voice.'

68 'Whatever a lover thinks they can do, that's what they'll try to do.'

73 'proof' means 'armoured'.

73 'enmity' means 'hatred'.

78 'proroguèd' means 'postponed'.

Theme — Love

Cupid is often shown as being blindfolded. This suggests that love doesn't follow reason, it's unpredictable. Shakespeare also refers to Cupid's blindness in Act 2, Scene 1 (lines 12-13).

Act 2, Scene 2

As that vast shore washed with the farthest sea,
I should adventure for such merchandise.

JULIET
Thou knowest the mask of night is on my face,
Else would a maiden blush bepaint my cheek
For that which thou hast heard me speak tonight.
Fain would I dwell on form, fain, fain deny
What I have spoke, but farewell compliment.
Dost thou love me? I know thou wilt say 'Ay',
And I will take thy word; yet if thou swear'st,
Thou mayst prove false: at lovers' perjuries
They say Jove laughs. O gentle Romeo,
If thou dost love, pronounce it faithfully.
Or if thou think'st I am too quickly won,
I'll frown and be perverse, and say thee nay,
So thou wilt woo, but else not for the world.
In truth, fair Montague, I am too fond,
And therefore thou mayst think my behaviour light:
But trust me, gentleman, I'll prove more true
Than those that have more coying to be strange.
I should have been more strange, I must confess,
But that thou overheard'st, ere I was ware,
My true-love passion — therefore pardon me,
And not impute this yielding to light love,
Which the dark night hath so discoverèd.

ROMEO
Lady, by yonder blessèd moon I vow,
That tips with silver all these fruit-tree tops —

JULIET
O swear not by the moon, th'inconstant moon,
That monthly changes in her circled orb,
Lest that thy love prove likewise variable.

ROMEO
What shall I swear by?

JULIET
Do not swear at all.
Or if thou wilt, swear by thy gracious self,
Which is the god of my idolatry,
And I'll believe thee.

ROMEO
If my heart's dear love —

JULIET
Well, do not swear. Although I joy in thee,
I have no joy of this contract tonight,
It is too rash, too unadvised, too sudden,
Too like the lightning, which doth cease to be
Ere one can say 'It lightens'. Sweet, good night.
This bud of love, by summer's ripening breath,
May prove a beauteous flower when next we meet.
Good night, good night! As sweet repose and rest
Come to thy heart as that within my breast.

ROMEO
O wilt thou leave me so unsatisfied?

JULIET
What satisfaction canst thou have tonight?

ROMEO
Th'exchange of thy love's faithful vow for mine.

JULIET
I gave thee mine before thou didst request it,
And yet I would it were to give again.

82-84 'I am not a sailor, but even if you were as far away as the shore of the furthest away sea, I would risk the journey for you'.

88-89 'I'd gladly act properly and deny what I've just said, but never mind good manners.'

92-93 'They say that the god Jove laughs at lies told by lovers.'

102 'more strange' means 'less open'. In other words, Juliet thinks she shouldn't have declared her love so openly.

Theme — Love

Romeo tries to treat love as a game and use poetry, but Juliet refuses — she wants to be straightforward about her feelings.

114 'idolatry' means 'worshipping an idol instead of God'.

Shakespeare's Techniques

Shakespeare often uses images of light to describe their relationship. Romeo compares Juliet to the sun in line 3, but Juliet compares their love to lightning, to show how quick it is.

Act 2, Scene 2

exits and entrances interrupt and frustrate Romeo & Juliet — audience also frustrated

ROMEO Wouldst thou withdraw it? For what purpose, love?

JULIET But to be frank and give it thee again,
And yet I wish but for the thing I have.
My bounty is as boundless as the sea,
My love as deep; the more I give to thee
The more I have, for both are infinite.

NURSE calls within ← behind the scenery

seperates them again

I hear some noise within. Dear love, adieu! —
Anon, good Nurse! Sweet Montague, be true.
Stay but a little, I will come again.

Exit above

ROMEO O blessèd, blessèd night! I am afeard,
Being in night, all this is but a dream,
Too flattering-sweet to be substantial.

Enter JULIET *above*

JULIET Three words, dear Romeo, and good night indeed.
If that thy bent of love be honourable,
Thy purpose marriage, send me word tomorrow,
By one that I'll procure to come to thee,
Where and what time thou wilt perform the rite,
And all my fortunes at thy foot I'll lay,
And follow thee my lord throughout the world.

NURSE (*Within*) Madam!

JULIET I come, anon. But if thou meanest not well,
I do beseech thee —

NURSE (*Within*) Madam!

JULIET By and by I come —
To cease thy strife, and leave me to my grief.
Tomorrow will I send.

ROMEO So thrive my soul —

JULIET A thousand times good night!

Exit above

ROMEO A thousand times the worse, to want thy light.
Love goes toward love as schoolboys from their books,
But love from love, toward school with heavy looks.

Retiring slowly

Enter JULIET *again (above)*

JULIET Hist, Romeo, hist! O for a falconer's voice,
To lure this tassel-gentle back again.
Bondage is hoarse, and may not speak aloud,
Else would I tear the cave where Echo lies,
And make her airy tongue more hoarse than mine
With repetition of my Romeo's name.

ROMEO It is my soul that calls upon my name.
How silver-sweet sound lovers' tongues by night,
Like softest music to attending ears!

JULIET Romeo!

We literally see that she is torn between her family and Romeo.

Shakespeare's Techniques

Juliet's repeated exits and the Nurse's interruptions make the scene (and Romeo and Juliet's love) seem tense and risky — they could get caught at any moment.

141 'too wonderful to be real.'

Character— Juliet

Juliet suggests they get married. This shows that despite her youth she's decisive.

151 'beseech' means 'beg'.

Shakespeare's Techniques

Shakespeare uses falconry metaphors — e.g. 'tassel-gentle' (a falcon) and 'niësse' (a young hawk) — to show that there's a strong bond between Juliet and Romeo, like the one between a bird and its falconer.

158 'Hist' is how a falconer calls to his bird.

160 'Bondage is hoarse' means 'prisoners must whisper'.

Act 2, Scene 2

ROMEO My niësse?

JULIET What o'clock tomorrow
Shall I send to thee?

ROMEO By the hour of nine.

JULIET I will not fail, 'tis twenty year till then.
I have forgot why I did call thee back.

ROMEO Let me stand here till thou remember it.

JULIET I shall forget, to have thee still stand there,
Remembering how I love thy company.

ROMEO And I'll still stay, to have thee still forget,
Forgetting any other home but this.

JULIET 'Tis almost morning, I would have thee gone,
And yet no farther than a wanton's bird,
That lets it hop a little from his hand,
Like a poor prisoner in his twisted gyves,
And with a silken thread plucks it back again,
So loving-jealous of his liberty.

ROMEO I would I were thy bird.

JULIET Sweet, so would I,
Yet I should kill thee with much cherishing.
Good night, good night! Parting is such sweet sorrow,
That I shall say good night till it be morrow.

Exit above

ROMEO Sleep dwell upon thine eyes, peace in thy breast!
Would I were sleep and peace, so sweet to rest!
Hence will I to my ghostly sire's close cell,
His help to crave, and my dear hap to tell.

Exit

177 'wanton' means 'spoilt child'.

179 'twisted gyves' means 'shackles'.

181 'loving, but jealous of his freedom'.

183 'much cherishing' means 'too much love'.

188 By 'ghostly sire' he means Friar Lawrence.

189 'dear hap' means 'good fortune'.

Shakespeare's Techniques

Juliet continues to use bird imagery. She compares her feelings for Romeo to a child who loves a bird too much for the bird's own good.

Performance

Because plays were performed during the day (see p.2), Shakespeare had to use language to set the scene. In Act 2, Scene 2, Juliet comments that Romeo is "bescreened in night" — this makes it clear to the audience that the action is taking place in the dark.

© Donald Cooper

Act 2, Scene 3 — Romeo Plans the Wedding

© Donald Cooper

Friar Lawrence opens the scene with a soliloquy while he gathers flowers and herbs. Romeo visits Friar Lawrence and asks the Friar to marry him to Juliet. Although Friar Lawrence isn't sure whether Romeo and Juliet are really in love, he agrees to marry them because he thinks it might end their families' feud.

ACT 2, SCENE 3

FRIAR LAWRENCE'S CELL

Enter FRIAR LAWRENCE, *with a basket*

FRIAR LAWRENCE The grey-eyed morn smiles on the frowning night,
Chequering the eastern clouds with streaks of light,
And flecked darkness like a drunkard reels
From forth day's path and Titan's fiery wheels.
Now, ere the sun advance his burning eye,
The day to cheer and night's dank dew to dry,
I must upfill this osier cage of ours
With baleful weeds and precious-juicèd flowers.
The earth that's nature's mother is her tomb,
What is her burying grave that is her womb,
And from her womb children of divers kind
We sucking on her natural bosom find,
Many for many virtues excellent,
None but for some and yet all different.
O, mickle is the powerful grace that lies
In herbs, plants, stones, and their true qualities.
For nought so vile that on the earth doth live
But to the earth some special good doth give,
Nor aught so good but strained from that fair use
Revolts from true birth, stumbling on abuse.
Virtue itself turns vice, being misapplied,
And vice sometimes by action dignified.

Enter ROMEO

Within the infant rind of this small flower
Poison hath residence and medicine power:
For this, being smelt, with that part cheers each part,
Being tasted, slays all senses with the heart.
Two such opposèd kings encamp them still
In man as well as herbs, grace and rude will —
And where the worser is predominant,
Full soon the canker death eats up that plant.

ROMEO Good morrow, father.

FRIAR LAWRENCE Benedicite!
What early tongue so sweet saluteth me?
Young son, it argues a distempered head
So soon to bid good morrow to thy bed.
Care keeps his watch in every old man's eye,
And where care lodges, sleep will never lie,

Shakespeare's Techniques

Friar Lawrence's soliloquy is full of opposites — 'smile' / 'frown', 'day' / 'night', 'grave' / 'womb', echoing the conflicts in the play.

7 'osier cage' means 'willow basket'.

8 'baleful' means 'poisonous'.

Character — Friar Lawrence

The first time we see Friar Lawrence, it's shown that he's an expert on the uses of plants as poisons and medicines. This hints at his role in the climax of the play.

15 'mickle' means 'great'.

Shakespeare's Techniques

Friar Lawrence remarks that herbs can both heal and kill. This foreshadows the tragic events at the end of the play.

25 In other words, 'If you smell this you'll feel better all over'.

30 'canker death' can mean 'cancerous death' or 'worm of death'.

31 'Benedicite' means 'bless you'.

33 'distempered' means 'disturbed'.

Act 2, Scene 3

Character — Friar Lawrence

The Friar calls Romeo 'good son' and 'pupil mine'. This shows that they have a close relationship.

45 'ghostly' means 'holy'.

Theme — Conflict

Romeo compares falling in love to being wounded. This suggests how love and conflict are connected.

54 'My request helps my enemy.'

55-56 In other words, 'Speak clearer Romeo — an unclear confession only receives muddled forgiveness.'

69 'brine' means 'tears'.

70 'sallow' means 'sickly yellow'.

80 'Women can't be expected to be faithful when men are so fickle.'

81 'You told me off for loving Rosaline'.

Character — Romeo

The Friar says Romeo's feelings for Rosaline were over the top. This emphasises how impulsive and changeable Romeo's emotions are.

But where unbruisèd youth with unstuffed brain
Doth couch his limbs, there golden sleep doth reign.
Therefore thy earliness doth me assure
Thou art uproused by some distemperature;
Or if not so, then here I hit it right,
Our Romeo hath not been in bed tonight.

ROMEO That last is true; the sweeter rest was mine.

FRIAR LAWRENCE God pardon sin! Wast thou with Rosaline?

ROMEO With Rosaline, my ghostly father? No.
I have forgot that name, and that name's woe.

FRIAR LAWRENCE That's my good son: but where
hast thou been, then?

ROMEO I'll tell thee, ere thou ask it me again.
I have been feasting with mine enemy,
Where on a sudden one hath wounded me,
That's by me wounded. Both our remedies
Within thy help and holy physic lies.
I bear no hatred, blessèd man, for, lo,
My intercession likewise steads my foe.

FRIAR LAWRENCE Be plain, good son, and homely in thy drift;
Riddling confession finds but riddling shrift.

ROMEO Then plainly know my heart's dear love is set
On the fair daughter of rich Capulet:
As mine on hers, so hers is set on mine;
And all combined, save what thou must combine
By holy marriage. When and where and how
We met, we wooed and made exchange of vow,
I'll tell thee as we pass, but this I pray,
That thou consent to marry us today.

FRIAR LAWRENCE Holy Saint Francis, what a change is here!
Is Rosaline, whom thou didst love so dear,
So soon forsaken? Young men's love then lies
Not truly in their hearts, but in their eyes.
Jesu Maria, what a deal of brine
Hath washed thy sallow cheeks for Rosaline!
How much salt water thrown away in waste,
To season love, that of it doth not taste!
The sun not yet thy sighs from heaven clears,
Thy old groans ring yet in my ancient ears.
Lo, here upon thy cheek the stain doth sit
Of an old tear that is not washed off yet.
If e'er thou wast thyself and these woes thine,
Thou and these woes were all for Rosaline:
And art thou changed? Pronounce this sentence then,
Women may fall, when there's no strength in men.

ROMEO Thou chid'st me oft for loving Rosaline.

FRIAR LAWRENCE For doting, not for loving, pupil mine.

ROMEO And bad'st me bury love.

FRIAR LAWRENCE Not in a grave,

Act 2, Scene 4 — Romeo Tells the Nurse

	To lay one in, another out to have.
ROMEO	I pray thee, chide not. She whom I love now Doth grace for grace and love for love allow; The other did not so.
FRIAR LAWRENCE	O, she knew well Thy love did read by rote and could not spell. But come, young waverer, come, go with me, In one respect I'll thy assistant be. For this alliance may so happy prove, To turn your households' rancour to pure love.
ROMEO	O, let us hence — I stand on sudden haste.
FRIAR LAWRENCE	Wisely and slow, they stumble that run fast.
	Exeunt

Character — Friar Lawrence

The Friar doesn't believe that Romeo loves Juliet, but he's willing to marry them to try to end the feud. This could be seen as a reckless decision.

88 In other words, 'You acted like you were in love, but you didn't know what love meant.'

Benvolio and Mercutio share some jokes about Tybalt's challenge to Romeo and Romeo's obsession with Rosaline. The Nurse comes to see Romeo, and he tells her his plan to marry Juliet that day.

ACT 2, SCENE 4

A STREET

Enter BENVOLIO *and* MERCUTIO

MERCUTIO	Where the devil should this Romeo be? Came he not home tonight?
BENVOLIO	Not to his father's, I spoke with his man.
MERCUTIO	Why, that same pale hard-hearted wench, that Rosaline, Torments him so, that he will sure run mad.
BENVOLIO	Tybalt, the kinsman of old Capulet, Hath sent a letter to his father's house.
MERCUTIO	A challenge, on my life.
BENVOLIO	Romeo will answer it.
MERCUTIO	Any man that can write may answer a letter.
BENVOLIO	Nay, he will answer the letter's master, how he dares, being dared.
MERCUTIO	Alas poor Romeo! He is already dead, stabbed with a white wench's black eye, shot through the ear with a love-song, the very pin of his heart cleft with the blind bow-boy's butt-shaft. And is he a man to encounter Tybalt?
BENVOLIO	Why, what is Tybalt?
MERCUTIO	More than Prince of Cats, I can tell you. O, he's the courageous captain of compliments. He fights as you sing prick-song, keeps time, distance, and proportion. He rests his minim rest, one, two, and the third in your bosom: the very butcher of a silk button, a duellist, a duellist, a gentleman of the very first house, of the first

Theme — Conflict

This scene opens with the news that Tybalt has challenged Romeo to a duel. This reminds the audience how dangerous Romeo's actions are.

Shakespeare's Techniques

Mercutio and the other characters are speaking in prose. This shows they're in a lighthearted mood despite the news of Tybalt's challenge.

15-16 In other words, 'Cupid's arrow'.

18 Tibalt was the name for the 'Prince of Cats' — a character in a set of well-known old stories.

20 'prick-song' means 'music sung very accurately'.

Act 2, Scene 4

24-25 'passado' and 'punto reverso' are sword-fighting moves.

27 'affecting phantasimes' means 'ridiculous young men'.

27-34 Mercutio is saying that he hates ridiculous people who use foreign expressions and fake accents, and he mocks the kinds of things they say.

36-37 Something like, 'Without Rosaline, Romeo looks skinny and pale, like a fish.'

Shakespeare's Techniques

Mercutio compares the object of Romeo's affection to other famous women like 'Dido', 'Thisbe' and 'Cleopatra'. These comparisons are ironic because all these characters had love affairs that ended badly.

43 'French slop' means 'loose trousers'.

47-48 'it was important, so it seemed okay to be impolite'.

50 'hams' means 'legs'.

57 'pump' means 'shoe'.

Shakespeare's Techniques

The comical word-play in this scene contrasts with the seriousness of the previous scenes and provides some light relief for the audience.

62 'I can't think of any more jokes'.

66-67 'Are we even now?'.

and second cause. Ah, the immortal passado, the punto reverso, the hai!

BENVOLIO The what?

MERCUTIO The pox of such antic, lisping, affecting phantasimes; these new tuners of accents! 'By Jesu, a very good blade, a very tall man, a very good whore!' Why, is not this a lamentable thing, grandsire, that we should be thus afflicted with these strange flies, these fashion-mongers, these pardon-me's, who stand so much on the new form, that they cannot sit at ease on the old bench? O, their bones, their bones!

Enter ROMEO

BENVOLIO Here comes Romeo, here comes Romeo.

MERCUTIO Without his roe, like a dried herring: O flesh, flesh, how art thou fishified! Now is he for the numbers that Petrarch flowed in. Laura to his lady was but a kitchen wench — marry, she had a better love to berhyme her, Dido a dowdy; Cleopatra a gipsy, Helen and Hero hildings and harlots, Thisbe a grey eye or so, but not to the purpose. Signior Romeo, bonjour! There's a French salutation to your French slop. You gave us the counterfeit fairly last night.

ROMEO Good morrow to you both. What counterfeit did I give you?

MERCUTIO The slip, sir, the slip. Can you not conceive?

ROMEO Pardon, good Mercutio, my business was great, and in such a case as mine a man may strain courtesy.

MERCUTIO That's as much as to say, such a case as yours constrains a man to bow in the hams.

ROMEO Meaning, to curtsy.

MERCUTIO Thou hast most kindly hit it.

ROMEO A most courteous exposition.

MERCUTIO Nay, I am the very pink of courtesy.

ROMEO Pink for flower.

MERCUTIO Right.

ROMEO Why, then is my pump well flowered.

MERCUTIO Sure wit! Follow me this jest now till thou hast worn out thy pump, that when the single sole of it is worn, the jest may remain after the wearing solely singular.

ROMEO O single-soled jest, solely singular for the singleness.

MERCUTIO Come between us, good Benvolio, my wits faint.

ROMEO Switch and spurs, switch and spurs, or I'll cry a match.

MERCUTIO Nay, if our wits run the wild goose chase, I am done, for thou hast more of the wild goose in one of thy wits than, I am sure, I have in my whole five. Was I with you there for the goose?

ROMEO Thou wast never with me for anything when thou

Act 2, Scene 4

wast not there for the goose.

MERCUTIO I will bite thee by the ear for that jest.

ROMEO Nay, good goose, bite not.

MERCUTIO Thy wit is a very bitter sweeting; it is a most sharp sauce.

ROMEO And is it not then well served in to a sweet goose?

MERCUTIO O here's a wit of cheveril, that stretches from an inch narrow to an ell broad!

ROMEO I stretch it out for that word 'broad', which added to the goose, proves thee far and wide a broad goose.

MERCUTIO Why, is not this better now than groaning for love? Now art thou sociable, now art thou Romeo; now art thou what thou art, by art as well as by nature. For this drivelling love is like a great natural, that runs lolling up and down to hide his bauble in a hole.

BENVOLIO Stop there, stop there.

MERCUTIO Thou desirest me to stop in my tale against the hair.

BENVOLIO Thou wouldst else have made thy tale large.

MERCUTIO O, thou art deceived — I would have made it short, for I was come to the whole depth of my tale; and meant, indeed, to occupy the argument no longer.

ROMEO Here's goodly gear!

Enter NURSE *and* PETER

MERCUTIO A sail, a sail!

BENVOLIO Two, two; a shirt and a smock.

NURSE Peter!

PETER Anon!

NURSE My fan, Peter.

MERCUTIO Good Peter, to hide her face, for her fan's the fairer face.

NURSE God ye good morrow, gentlemen.

MERCUTIO God ye good den, fair gentlewoman.

NURSE Is it good den?

MERCUTIO 'Tis no less, I tell you, for the bawdy hand of the dial is now upon the prick of noon.

NURSE Out upon you! What a man are you!

ROMEO One, gentlewoman, that God hath made for himself to mar.

NURSE By my troth, it is well said; 'for himself to mar,' quoth 'a? Gentlemen, can any of you tell me where I may find the young Romeo?

ROMEO I can tell you, but young Romeo will be older when you have found him than he was when you sought him. I am the youngest of that name, for fault of a worse.

NURSE You say well.

MERCUTIO Yea, is the worst well? Very well took, i'faith. Wisely, wisely.

NURSE If you be he, sir, I desire some confidence with you.

---

70 'jest' means 'joke'.

74-75 'Here's a joke of leather, that has been stretched from an inch to a yard wide'. Mercutio is saying that Romeo has done the joke to death.

Character — Romeo

Mercutio suggests that Romeo's playful side is the real Romeo. Rosaline made him glum, but Juliet has made him happy again.

81-82 'this foolish love is like a great idiot, that runs up and down, looking to hide his toy in a hole.'

84 In other words, 'before it's done'.

90-91 Mercutio and Benvolio make a joke about the Nurse's clothes being as large as a ship's sail.

97 'good den' means 'good afternoon'.

103 'quoth' means 'said'.

Act 2, Scene 4

113 'bawd' means 'brothel-keeper' or 'hare'.

Character — Mercutio

Mercutio is always making crude jokes about sex. He can't resist punning and twisting people's words.

BENVOLIO She will indite him to some supper.

MERCUTIO A bawd, a bawd, a bawd! So ho!

ROMEO What hast thou found?

MERCUTIO No hare, sir, unless a hare, sir, in a lenten pie, that is something stale and hoar ere it be spent.
(*Sings*) An old hare hoar
And an old hare hoar,
Is very good meat in Lent
But a hare that is hoar
Is too much for a score,
When it hoars ere it be spent.
Romeo, will you come to your father's?
We'll to dinner, thither.

ROMEO I will follow you.

MERCUTIO Farewell, ancient lady; farewell (*Singing*) 'lady, lady, lady.'

Exeunt MERCUTIO *and* BENVOLIO

127-128 'tell me who that rude man was'

128 'ropery' means 'crude jokes'.

NURSE Marry, farewell! I pray you, sir, what saucy merchant was this, that was so full of his ropery?

ROMEO A gentleman, Nurse, that loves to hear himself talk, and will speak more in a minute than he will stand to in a month.

135 'flirt-gills' means 'flirts' and 'skains-mates' means 'bloodthirsty friends'.

NURSE And 'a speak any thing against me, I'll take him down, and 'a were lustier than he is, and twenty such Jacks; and if I cannot, I'll find those that shall. Scurvy knave! I am none of his flirt-gills, I am none of his skains-mates. And thou must stand by too, and suffer every knave to use me at his pleasure?

PETER I saw no man use you at his pleasure; if I had, my weapon should quickly have been out, I warrant you, I dare draw as soon as another man, if I see occasion in a good quarrel, and the law on my side.

Character — Nurse

The Nurse warns Romeo not to take advantage of Juliet. This shows how protective she is of Juliet.

NURSE Now, afore God, I am so vexed, that every part about me quivers. Scurvy knave! Pray you, sir, a word — and as I told you, my young lady bid me enquire you out; what she bid me say, I will keep to myself. But first let me tell ye, if ye should lead her into a fool's paradise, as they say, it were a very gross kind of behaviour, as they say: for the gentlewoman is young; and, therefore, if you should deal double with her, truly it were an ill thing to be offered to any gentlewoman, and very weak dealing.

152 'send my greetings to Juliet'.

ROMEO Nurse, commend me to thy lady and mistress. I protest unto thee —

154 'i'faith' means 'indeed'.

NURSE Good heart, and, i'faith, I will tell her as much. Lord, Lord, she will be a joyful woman.

156 'mark' means 'pay attention to'.

ROMEO What wilt thou tell her, Nurse? Thou dost not mark me.

157 The Nurse gets confused between 'protest' and 'propose'.

NURSE I will tell her, sir, that you do protest — which, as I take it, is a gentlemanlike offer.

Act 2, Scene 4

dramatic irony - we know the marriage will lead to a suicide

ROMEO Bid her devise
Some means to come to shrift this afternoon; → confession
And there she shall at Friar Lawrence' cell
Be shrived and married. Here is for thy pains.

NURSE No truly sir, not a penny.

ROMEO Go to, I say you shall.

NURSE This afternoon, sir? Well, she shall be there.

ROMEO And stay, good Nurse, behind the abbey wall.
Within this hour my man shall be with thee,
And bring thee cords made like a tackled stair,
Which to the high top-gallant of my joy
Must be my convoy in the secret night.
Farewell, be trusty, and I'll quit thy pains:
Farewell, commend me to thy mistress.

NURSE Now God in heaven bless thee! Hark you, sir.

ROMEO What say'st thou, my dear Nurse?

NURSE Is your man secret? Did you ne'er hear say,
Two may keep counsel, putting one away?

ROMEO I warrant thee, my man's as true as steel.

NURSE Well, sir, my mistress is the sweetest lady. Lord, Lord! when 'twas a little prating thing — O, there is a nobleman in town, one Paris, that would fain lay knife aboard; but she, good soul, had as lief see a toad, a very toad, as see him. I anger her sometimes and tell her that Paris is the properer man, but, I'll warrant you, when I say so, she looks as pale as any clout in the versal world. Doth not rosemary and Romeo begin both with a letter?

ROMEO Ay, Nurse, what of that? Both with an R.

NURSE Ah, mocker! That's the dog's name; R is for the — No, I know it begins with some other letter — and she hath the prettiest sententious of it, of you and rosemary, that it would do you good to hear it.

ROMEO Commend me to thy lady.

NURSE Ay, a thousand times.

Exit ROMEO

Peter!

PETER Anon!

NURSE Peter, take my fan, and go before and apace.

Exeunt

Shakespeare won't let us forget that Juliet's father wants her to marry Paris

159-160 'Ask her to find some excuse to go to confession.'

Shakespeare's Techniques

Romeo switches to blank verse when he starts to talk about his wedding plans. This shows how serious he is about Juliet.

167-170 In other words, 'Within an hour, my servant will bring you a rope ladder, which I will use to climb into Juliet's bedroom this evening.'

175-176 Something like, 'Can you trust your man? Did you never hear the saying "Two can keep a secret if one doesn't know it"?'

Shakespeare's Techniques

The Nurse tells Romeo that Paris is also interested in Juliet. This hints that Romeo and Juliet's marriage might be affected by the other characters.

184-185 In other words, 'she goes as white as a sheet.'

189-190 'she has the prettiest things to say about you'.

195 'apace' means 'quickly'.

Act 2, Scene 5 — Juliet Learns of Romeo's Plan

Juliet is at home, impatiently waiting for the Nurse to return with news from Romeo. The Nurse teases Juliet and then tells her about the wedding arrangements.

Character — Juliet

Juliet is on edge waiting for word from Romeo. This shows her immaturity, but also increases the play's excitement — everything is happening quickly.

6 'lowering' means 'gloomy'.

7 'nimble-pinioned' means 'swift-winged'.

14 'bandy' means 'knock back and forth'.

16 'feign' means 'pretend'.

22-24 'Even if it's bad news, tell me it cheerfully. If it's good, you'll spoil it with your sour face'.

26 'jaunce' means 'troublesome journey'.

Character — Juliet

The playful way that Juliet talks to the Nurse shows how close they are. This contrasts with the formal way that she speaks to her parents.

ACT 2, SCENE 5

CAPULET'S ORCHARD

Enter JULIET

JULIET
The clock struck nine when I did send the Nurse,
In half an hour she promised to return.
Perchance she cannot meet him: that's not so.
O, she is lame! Love's heralds should be thoughts,
Which ten times faster glide than the sun's beams,
Driving back shadows over lowering hills.
Therefore do nimble-pinioned doves draw love,
And therefore hath the wind-swift Cupid wings.
Now is the sun upon the highmost hill
Of this day's journey, and from nine till twelve
Is three long hours, yet she is not come.
Had she affections and warm youthful blood,
She would be as swift in motion as a ball;
My words would bandy her to my sweet love,
And his to me.
But old folks, many feign as they were dead,
Unwieldy, slow, heavy and pale as lead.
O God, she comes!

Enter NURSE *and* PETER

O honey nurse, what news?
Hast thou met with him? Send thy man away.

NURSE
Peter, stay at the gate.

Exit PETER

JULIET
Now, good sweet Nurse — O Lord, why look'st thou sad?
Though news be sad, yet tell them merrily,
If good, thou shamest the music of sweet news
By playing it to me with so sour a face.

NURSE
I am a-weary, give me leave awhile.
Fie, how my bones ache! What a jaunce have I!

JULIET
I would thou hadst my bones, and I thy news:
Nay, come, I pray thee, speak, good, good Nurse, speak.

NURSE
Jesu, what haste? Can you not stay awhile?
Do you not see that I am out of breath?

JULIET
How art thou out of breath, when thou hast breath
To say to me that thou art out of breath?
The excuse that thou dost make in this delay
Is longer than the tale thou dost excuse.

Act 2, Scene 5

Is thy news good, or bad? Answer to that.
Say either, and I'll stay the circumstance.
Let me be satisfied, is't good or bad?

NURSE Well, you have made a simple choice. You know not how to choose a man. Romeo? No, not he; though his face be better than any man's, yet his leg excels all men's, and for a hand, and a foot, and a body, though they be not to be talked on, yet they are past compare. He is not the flower of courtesy, but, I'll warrant him, as gentle as a lamb. Go thy ways, wench, serve God. What, have you dined at home?

JULIET No, no. But all this did I know before.
What says he of our marriage? What of that?

NURSE Lord, how my head aches! What a head have I!
It beats as it would fall in twenty pieces.
My back o' t'other side — O, my back, my back!
Beshrew your heart for sending me about,
To catch my death with jauncing up and down!

JULIET I'faith, I am sorry that thou art not well.
Sweet, sweet, sweet Nurse, tell me, what says my love?

NURSE Your love says, like an honest gentleman, and a courteous, and a kind, and a handsome, and, I warrant, a virtuous — Where is your mother?

JULIET Where is my mother! Why, she is within;
Where should she be? How oddly thou repliest!
'Your love says, like an honest gentleman,
"Where is your mother?"'

NURSE O God's lady dear!
Are you so hot? Marry, come up, I trow.
Is this the poultice for my aching bones?
Henceforward do your messages yourself.

JULIET Here's such a coil! Come, what says Romeo?

NURSE Have you got leave to go to shrift today?

JULIET I have.

NURSE Then hie you hence to Friar Lawrence' cell.
There stays a husband to make you a wife.
Now comes the wanton blood up in your cheeks,
They'll be in scarlet straight at any news.
Hie you to church; I must another way,
To fetch a ladder, by the which your love
Must climb a bird's nest soon when it is dark.
I am the drudge and toil in your delight,
But you shall bear the burden soon at night.
Go — I'll to dinner, hie you to the cell.

JULIET Hie to high fortune! Honest Nurse, farewell.

Exeunt

36 'I'll wait for the details.'

38 'simple' means 'foolish'.

Character — Nurse

The Nurse teases Juliet by focusing on Romeo's sex appeal. This echoes Mercutio's speech about Rosaline in Act 2 Scene 1. The Nurse and Mercutio share a rude sense of humour.

51 'Beshrew' means 'curse'.

62 'hot' means 'impatient'.

65 'coil' means 'fuss'.

Character — Juliet

Juliet's parents allow her to visit Friar Lawrence's cell alone for confession, but she uses this freedom to go and marry Romeo. This is the first example of Juliet disobeying her parents.

68 'hie' means 'go quickly'.

Act 2, Scene 6 — Romeo and Juliet Marry

Friar Lawrence warns Romeo about getting married too quickly — although the Friar is keen to get the wedding underway. Juliet meets Romeo and the Friar at the Friar's cell and they head off to church.

1-2 'May heaven smile on this marriage, so that there is no future sorrow to make us regret it.'

4 'countervail' means 'outweigh'.

Theme — Fate

This is dramatic irony — it's as if he's tempting fate. The audience knows that Romeo and Juliet will die.

Shakespeare's Techniques

The Friar's contrasting language 'triumph' / 'die', 'loathsome' / 'delicious' foreshadows how Romeo and Juliet's happiness will soon be contrasted with misery.

15 'Too fast is as bad as too slow'.

17 Something like, 'Will never survive the rockiness of life'.

18-20 'A lover can walk along a fine cobweb that blows in the playful summer air, and yet not fall — so flimsy is their earthly pleasure'.

26 'blazon' means 'beautifully describe'.

30-31 In other words, 'True understanding is richer than words. It has real meaning — it isn't just decoration.'

Shakespeare's Techniques

This scene is very brief and hurried. This matches the frantic pace of Romeo and Juliet's relationship.

ACT 2, SCENE 6

FRIAR LAWRENCE'S CELL

Enter FRIAR LAWRENCE *and* ROMEO

FRIAR LAWRENCE So smile the heavens upon this holy act,
That after hours with sorrow chide us not!

ROMEO Amen, amen! But come what sorrow can,
It cannot countervail the exchange of joy
That one short minute gives me in her sight.
Do thou but close our hands with holy words,
Then love-devouring death do what he dare,
It is enough I may but call her mine.

FRIAR LAWRENCE These violent delights have violent ends
And in their triumph die, like fire and powder,
Which as they kiss consume: the sweetest honey
Is loathsome in his own deliciousness
And in the taste confounds the appetite.
Therefore love moderately, long love doth so;
Too swift arrives as tardy as too slow.

Enter JULIET

Here comes the lady. O, so light a foot
Will ne'er wear out the everlasting flint.
A lover may bestride the gossamers
That idles in the wanton summer air,
And yet not fall; so light is vanity.

JULIET Good even to my ghostly confessor.

FRIAR LAWRENCE Romeo shall thank thee, daughter, for us both.

JULIET As much to him, else is his thanks too much.

ROMEO Ah, Juliet, if the measure of thy joy
Be heaped like mine and that thy skill be more
To blazon it, then sweeten with thy breath
This neighbour air, and let rich music's tongue
Unfold the imagined happiness that both
Receive in either by this dear encounter.

JULIET Conceit, more rich in matter than in words,
Brags of his substance, not of ornament:
They are but beggars that can count their worth,
But my true love is grown to such excess
I cannot sum up sum of half my wealth.

FRIAR LAWRENCE Come, come with me, and we will make short work,
For, by your leaves, you shall not stay alone
Till holy church incorporate two in one.

Exeunt

Act Two — Practice Questions

Quick Questions

1) Where does Act 2, Scene 2 take place?

2) Give two examples of imagery from Act 2, Scene 2.

3) Why has Friar Lawrence got a basket at the beginning of Act 2, Scene 3?

4) What two possible reasons does Friar Lawrence give for Romeo being up so early?

5) Why does Friar Lawrence agree to marry Romeo and Juliet?

6) Give two examples of puns from Act 2, Scene 4.

7) Who does the Nurse describe as a "saucy merchant"?

8) How long is the Nurse away from Juliet, meeting Romeo?

9) How does Romeo intend to get into Juliet's room on their wedding night?

10) Find two adjectives that the Nurse uses to describe Romeo from Act 2, Scene 5.

In-depth Questions

1) How are Mercutio's and Romeo's views on love different?

2) Why do you think Romeo waits before he speaks to Juliet at the beginning of Act 2, Scene 2?

3) What does it tell you about Romeo and how he feels for Juliet that he uses imagery based on the heavens, the moon, the stars and the sun in Act 2, Scene 2?

4) Do you think Friar Lawrence is knowledgable about love? Explain your answer.

5) How would you describe Romeo's mood in Act 2, Scene 4? Give reasons for your answer.

6) Why do you think the Nurse delays telling Juliet her news in Act 2, Scene 5?

7) Why do you think Romeo and Juliet are married off stage?

8) Imagine you are a costume designer for a modern-day production of *Romeo and Juliet*. Describe what clothes you'd give Mercutio, and explain your choices.

Act 3, Scene 1 — Tybalt and Mercutio are Killed

The Montagues and the Capulets run into each other. Tybalt wants to fight Romeo, but Romeo refuses. Mercutio provokes Tybalt and they start to fight. Romeo tries to break them up, but Tybalt stabs and kills Mercutio under Romeo's arm. Romeo kills Tybalt in revenge and then flees. The Prince banishes Romeo as punishment.

up until this scene, the play could have been a romantic comedy. After, two murders, it is now a tragedy

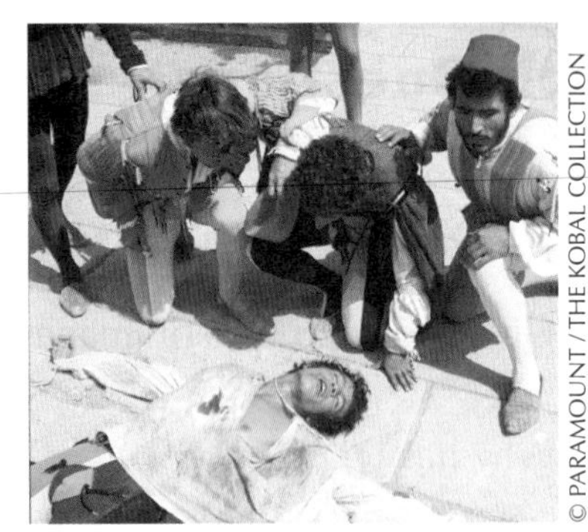

ACT 3, SCENE 1

A 'page' was a boy servant.

2 'Capels' means 'Capulets'.

3 'scape' means 'escape'.

Shakespeare's Techniques

Benvolio's language is violent and sinister. His warning creates a tense atmosphere.

9 'drawer' means 'barman'.

11-13 'Come on, you can be as angry as anyone in Italy when you're in the mood. You're easily angered, and when you're not angry you soon find something to be angry about.'

Shakespeare's Techniques

This aggressive, violent scene contrasts with the hopeful, romantic ending of Act 2. This switch in atmosphere makes the play more dramatic.

27 A 'doublet' is a kind of jacket.

28 'riband' means 'ribbon'.

30-31 Benvolio is saying that if he was as argumentative as Mercutio, then his life wouldn't be worth very much — because he'd be dead very quickly.

33 'By my head' means 'oh dear'.

VERONA. A PUBLIC PLACE.

Enter MERCUTIO *and his* PAGE, BENVOLIO, *and men*

BENVOLIO I pray thee, good Mercutio, let's retire:
The day is hot, the Capels are abroad,
And if we meet we shall not scape a brawl,
For now, these hot days, is the mad blood stirring.

MERCUTIO Thou art like one of these fellows that, when he enters the confines of a tavern, claps me his sword upon the table, and says 'God send me no need of thee!'; and by the operation of the second cup draws him on the drawer, when indeed there is no need.

BENVOLIO Am I like such a fellow?

MERCUTIO Come, come, thou art as hot a Jack in thy mood as any in Italy, and as soon moved to be moody, and as soon moody to be moved.

BENVOLIO And what to?

MERCUTIO Nay, and there were two such, we should have none shortly, for one would kill the other. Thou? Why, thou wilt quarrel with a man that hath a hair more or a hair less in his beard than thou hast; thou wilt quarrel with a man for cracking nuts, having no other reason but because thou hast hazel eyes. What eye but such an eye would spy out such a quarrel? Thy head is as full of quarrels as an egg is full of meat, and yet thy head hath been beaten as addle as an egg for quarrelling. Thou hast quarrelled with a man for coughing in the street, because he hath wakened thy dog that hath lain asleep in the sun. Didst thou not fall out with a tailor for wearing his new doublet before Easter? With another for tying his new shoes with old riband? And yet thou wilt tutor me from quarrelling?

BENVOLIO And I were so apt to quarrel as thou art, any man should buy the fee-simple of my life for an hour and a quarter.

MERCUTIO The fee-simple? O simple!

Enter TYBALT, PETRUCHIO *and others*

BENVOLIO By my head, here comes the Capulets.

MERCUTIO By my heel, I care not.

Act 3, Scene 1

TYBALT Follow me close, for I will speak to them.
Gentlemen, good den, a word with one of you.

MERCUTIO And but one word with one of us? Couple it with something, make it a word and a blow.

TYBALT You shall find me apt enough to that, sir, and you will give me occasion.

MERCUTIO Could you not take some occasion without giving?

TYBALT Mercutio, thou consortest with Romeo.

MERCUTIO Consort? what, dost thou make us minstrels? And thou make minstrels of us, look to hear nothing but discords. Here's my fiddlestick, here's that shall make you dance. 'Zounds, consort!

BENVOLIO We talk here in the public haunt of men:
Either withdraw unto some private place,
Or reason coldly of your grievances,
Or else depart; here all eyes gaze on us.

MERCUTIO Men's eyes were made to look, and let them gaze;
I will not budge for no man's pleasure, I.

Enter ROMEO

TYBALT Well, peace be with you, sir, here comes my man.

MERCUTIO But I'll be hanged, sir, if he wear your livery,
Marry, go before to field, he'll be your follower;
Your worship in that sense may call him man.

TYBALT Romeo, the love I bear thee can afford
No better term than this: thou art a villain.

ROMEO Tybalt, the reason that I have to love thee
Doth much excuse the appertaining rage
To such a greeting. Villain am I none;
Therefore farewell, I see thou knowest me not.

TYBALT Boy, this shall not excuse the injuries
That thou hast done me, therefore turn and draw.

ROMEO I do protest I never injured thee,
But love thee better than thou canst devise,
Till thou shalt know the reason of my love;
And so, good Capulet, which name I tender
As dearly as mine own, be satisfied.

MERCUTIO O calm, dishonourable, vile submission!
'Alla stoccata' carries it away. (*Draws*)
Tybalt, you rat-catcher, will you walk?

TYBALT What wouldst thou have with me?

MERCUTIO Good King of Cats, nothing but one of your nine lives that I mean to make bold withal, and as you shall use me hereafter, dry-beat the rest of the eight. Will you pluck your sword out of his pilcher by the ears? Make haste, lest mine be about your ears ere it be out.

TYBALT I am for you. (*Drawing*)

ROMEO Gentle Mercutio, put thy rapier up.

Character — Mercutio

Tybalt is trying to be polite, but Mercutio wants to start a fight. This shows Mercutio's aggressive side.

42 'consortest' means 'are friends with'.

43 'consort' means 'a group of musicians'. Mercutio is twisting Tybalt's words.

43 'minstrels' means 'musicians'.

46 ''Zounds' is something like saying 'damn!'.

53 & 56 Tybalt calls Romeo 'my man' — Mercutio twists this to mean Tybalt's calling Romeo his 'servant'.

59-61 Something like, 'the reason I have for loving you stops me feeling the appropriate anger for such an insult.'

Shakespeare's Techniques

This is dramatic irony. The audience knows that Romeo is trying to avoid the fight because he's now related to Tybalt, but Mercutio and Tybalt think he's being cowardly.

71 'Alla stoccata' is a sword-fighting phrase. Mercutio is saying that he'll fight instead of Romeo.

76 'thrash the other eight lives out of you'.

77 A 'pilcher' is a scabbard.

80 'put thy rapier up' means 'put your sword away'.

Act 3, Scene 1

81 'passado' means 'sword thrust'.

Character — Romeo

Romeo is desperate to stop the fight. He is trying to protect them — Mercutio is his best friend and Tybalt is part of his new family.

87 'sped' means 'killed'.

Character — Mercutio

Even as he dies Mercutio makes a pun on "grave" (meaning 'serious' and 'a place to put dead bodies').

98 'fights as if he learnt it from a book'.

105 'ally' means 'relative'.

110-111 'Juliet's beauty has made me woman-like and has weakened my courage.'

Shakespeare's Techniques

When Mercutio dies the mood of the play changes. Mercutio provided much of the humour — after this scene the atmosphere is more tragic and serious.

115 Something like, 'will bring more bad days.'

MERCUTIO Come, sir, your 'passado'.

They fight

ROMEO Draw, Benvolio, beat down their weapons.
Gentlemen, for shame forbear this outrage!
Tybalt, Mercutio, the Prince expressly hath
Forbid this bandying in Verona streets.

ROMEO *steps between them*

Hold, Tybalt! Good Mercutio!

TYBALT *under* ROMEO*'s arm thrusts* MERCUTIO *in*
Away TYBALT *(with his followers)*

MERCUTIO I am hurt.
A plague a'both your houses! I am sped.
Is he gone and hath nothing?

BENVOLIO What, art thou hurt?

MERCUTIO Ay, ay, a scratch, a scratch, marry, 'tis enough.
Where is my page? Go, villain, fetch a surgeon.

Exit PAGE

ROMEO Courage, man, the hurt cannot be much.

MERCUTIO No, 'tis not so deep as a well, nor so wide as a church-door, but 'tis enough, 'twill serve. Ask for me tomorrow, and you shall find me a grave man. I am peppered, I warrant, for this world. A plague a'both your houses! 'Zounds, a dog, a rat, a mouse, a cat, to scratch a man to death! A braggart, a rogue, a villain, that fights by the book of arithmetic. Why the devil came you between us? I was hurt under your arm.

ROMEO I thought all for the best.

MERCUTIO Help me into some house, Benvolio,
Or I shall faint. A plague a'both your houses!
They have made worms' meat of me. I have it
And soundly too. Your houses!

Exit (with BENVOLIO*)*

ROMEO This gentleman, the Prince's near ally,
My very friend, hath got this mortal hurt
In my behalf; my reputation stained
With Tybalt's slander — Tybalt, that an hour
Hath been my cousin. O sweet Juliet,
Thy beauty hath made me effeminate,
And in my temper softened valour's steel!

Enter BENVOLIO

BENVOLIO O Romeo, Romeo, brave Mercutio is dead.
That gallant spirit hath aspired the clouds,
Which too untimely here did scorn the earth.

ROMEO This day's black fate on moe days doth depend,
This but begins the woe others must end.

Enter TYBALT

BENVOLIO Here comes the furious Tybalt back again.

Act 3, Scene 1

ROMEO Again, in triumph, and Mercutio slain?
Away to heaven, respective lenity,
And fire-eyed fury be my conduct now!
Now, Tybalt, take the 'villain' back again
That late thou gav'st me, for Mercutio's soul
Is but a little way above our heads,
Staying for thine to keep him company.
Either thou or I, or both, must go with him.

TYBALT Thou wretched boy, that didst consort him here,
Shalt with him hence.

ROMEO This shall determine that.

They fight — TYBALT *falls*

BENVOLIO Romeo, away, be gone!
The citizens are up, and Tybalt slain.
Stand not amazed, the Prince will doom thee death
If thou art taken. Hence be gone, away!

confused

ROMEO O, I am fortune's fool.

BENVOLIO Why dost thou stay?

Exit ROMEO

Enter Citizens (*as* OFFICERS *of the Watch*)

OFFICER Which way ran he that killed Mercutio?
Tybalt, that murderer, which way ran he?

BENVOLIO There lies that Tybalt.

OFFICER Up, sir, go with me;
I charge thee in the Prince's name obey.

Enter PRINCE, *old* MONTAGUE, CAPULET, *their* WIVES *and all*

everyone → a crowd of people

the families have all entered

PRINCE Where are the vile beginners of this fray?

BENVOLIO O noble Prince, I can discover all
The unlucky manage of this fatal brawl;
There lies the man, slain by young Romeo,
That slew thy kinsman, brave Mercutio.

LADY CAPULET Tybalt, my cousin! O my brother's child!
O Prince! O husband! O, the blood is spilled
Of my dear kinsman. Prince, as thou art true,
For blood of ours, shed blood of Montague.
O cousin, cousin!

execute Romeo

PRINCE Benvolio, who began this bloody fray?

BENVOLIO Tybalt, here slain, whom Romeo's hand did slay.
Romeo, that spoke him fair, bid him bethink
How nice the quarrel was, and urged withal
Your high displeasure; all this, utterèd
With gentle breath, calm look, knees humbly bowed,
Could not take truce with the unruly spleen
Of Tybalt deaf to peace, but that he tilts
With piercing steel at bold Mercutio's breast,
Who, all as hot, turns deadly point to point,
And with a martial scorn, with one hand beats
Cold death aside, and with the other sends

119 'respective lenity' means 'respectful gentleness'.

Character — Romeo

Romeo was trying to prevent a fight, but Mercutio's death has made him angry.

Theme — Fate

Romeo thinks he's been a victim of fate. It reminds the audience that "star-cross'd" Romeo has been doomed from the start.

137 'Where are the people that started this fight?'

139 'unlucky management'.

144-145 'Prince, kill Romeo for killing Tybalt'.

149 'spoke him fair' means 'spoke politely to him'.

150 'nice' means 'foolish'.

153 'unruly spleen' means 'anger'.

Act 3, Scene 1

It back to Tybalt, whose dexterity
Retorts it. Romeo he cries aloud,
'Hold, friends! Friends, part!' and swifter than his tongue,
His agile arm beats down their fatal points,
And 'twixt them rushes; underneath whose arm
An envious thrust from Tybalt hit the life
Of stout Mercutio, and then Tybalt fled;
But by and by comes back to Romeo,
Who had but newly entertained revenge,
And to't they go like lightning, for, ere I
Could draw to part them, was stout Tybalt slain;
And as he fell, did Romeo turn and fly.
This is the truth, or let Benvolio die.

LADY CAPULET He is a kinsman to the Montague,
Affection makes him false, he speaks not true:
Some twenty of them fought in this black strife,
And all those twenty could but kill one life.
I beg for justice, which thou, Prince, must give:
Romeo slew Tybalt, Romeo must not live.

PRINCE Romeo slew him, he slew Mercutio;
Who now the price of his dear blood doth owe?

MONTAGUE Not Romeo, Prince, he was Mercutio's friend;
His fault concludes but what the law should end,
The life of Tybalt.

PRINCE And for that offence
Immediately we do exile him hence.
I have an interest in your hearts' proceeding;
My blood for your rude brawls doth lie a-bleeding;
But I'll amerce you with so strong a fine
That you shall all repent the loss of mine.
I will be deaf to pleading and excuses,
Nor tears nor prayers shall purchase out abuses.
Therefore use none. Let Romeo hence in haste,
Else, when he is found, that hour is his last.
Bear hence this body, and attend our will:
Mercy but murders, pardoning those that kill.

Exeunt

165 'stout' means 'brave'.

167 'just started to think about revenge'.

172-175 'He's part of Romeo's family — he's lying. There were twenty of them and they still only just managed to kill Tybalt.'

Shakespeare's Techniques

The Prince often speaks in the first person plural ('we') and uses rhyming couplets. The Prince's very formal way of speaking sets him apart from the squabbling families.

Theme — Family

Mercutio was related to the Prince — his death shows how the feud is affecting other families. The violence is getting out of control.

186 'amerce' means 'punish'.

193 'Pardoning killers only leads to more murders.'

Shakespeare's view of Italy

Shakespeare set several of his plays in Italy — he often based them on Italian stories. People in England were interested in Italy — it was seen as an exotic and sophisticated country. But the characters in *Romeo and Juliet* reflect popular stereotypes of the day — Italians were seen as passionate, violent and lustful.

© PARAMOUNT / THE KOBAL COLLECTION

Act 3, Scene 2 — Juliet Gets Some Bad News

Juliet's waiting for Romeo to come and visit her that evening. The Nurse enters and tells Juliet that Romeo killed Tybalt and he's has been banished. Juliet is upset, so the Nurse says she will find Romeo for her.

ACT 3, SCENE 2

JULIET'S ROOM IN CAPULET'S MANSION

Enter JULIET *alone*

JULIET
Gallop apace, you fiery-footed steeds,
Towards Phoebus' lodging; such a wagoner
As Phaeton would whip you to the west,
And bring in cloudy night immediately.
Spread thy close curtain, love-performing night,
That runaways' eyes may wink, and Romeo
Leap to these arms, untalked of and unseen:
Lovers can see to do their amorous rites
By their own beauties, or if love be blind,
It best agrees with night. Come, civil night,
Thou sober-suited matron all in black,
And learn me how to lose a winning match,
Played for a pair of stainless maidenhoods.
Hood my unmanned blood, bating in my cheeks,
With thy black mantle, till strange love grow bold,
Think true love acted simple modesty.
Come, night, come, Romeo, come, thou day in night,
For thou wilt lie upon the wings of night,
Whiter than new snow upon a raven's back.
Come, gentle night, come, loving, black-browed night,
Give me my Romeo, and when I shall die,
Take him and cut him out in little stars,
And he will make the face of heaven so fine
That all the world will be in love with night,
And pay no worship to the garish sun.
O, I have bought the mansion of a love,
But not possessed it, and though I am sold,
Not yet enjoyed. So tedious is this day
As is the night before some festival
To an impatient child that hath new robes
And may not wear them. O, here comes my Nurse,

Enter NURSE, *with the ladder of cords in her lap*

And she brings news, and every tongue that speaks
But Romeo's name speaks heavenly eloquence.
Now, Nurse, what news? What hast thou there? The cords
That Romeo bid thee fetch?

NURSE
Ay, ay, the cords.

Throws them down

Shakespeare's Techniques

Romeo and Juliet's relationship is linked with darkness — the night-time balcony scene, this scene waiting for the sun to go down, and the final scene in the dark tomb. This emphasises how secret they have to keep their relationship.

12 'win Romeo by surrendering to him'.

13 'maidenhoods' means 'virginities'.

14-15 Something like, 'night, cover up my blushing cheeks with your black hood.'

15 'strange' means 'unfamiliar'.

Theme — Love

Juliet is excited about sleeping with Romeo. This makes their relationship more convincing — there's desire in their love.

34 'The cords' means 'the rope ladder'.

Act 3, Scene 2

37-39 The Nurse is upset because Tybalt's dead. Juliet's confused because it sounds like the Nurse means Romeo's dead.

38 'undone' means 'ruined'.

40 'envious' means 'spiteful' and 'jealous'.

45 'ay' means 'yes'.

47 A 'cockatrice' is a mythical creature which kills people by looking at them.

51 'weal' means 'well-being'.

Shakespeare's Techniques

The Nurse's gory language makes the scene more shocking.

54 'corse' means 'corpse'.

56 'sounded' means 'fainted'.

59-60 'Let me die too and join Romeo on the funeral bed.'

Shakespeare's Techniques

Juliet's questions and exclamations show her shock and confusion at the news.

66 'my dearer lord' means 'Romeo'.

Shakespeare's Techniques

Juliet uses oxymorons such as "damnèd saint" to show her conflicting feelings towards Romeo.

JULIET Ay me, what news? Why dost thou wring thy hands?

NURSE Ah weraday, he's dead, he's dead, he's dead!
We are undone, lady, we are undone.
Alack the day, he's gone, he's killed, he's dead!

JULIET Can heaven be so envious?

NURSE Romeo can,
Though heaven cannot. O Romeo, Romeo!
Who ever would have thought it? Romeo!

JULIET What devil art thou that dost torment me thus?
This torture should be roared in dismal hell.
Hath Romeo slain himself? Say thou but 'ay'
And that bare vowel 'I' shall poison more
Than the death-darting eye of cockatrice.
I am not I, if there be such an 'ay',
Or those eyes shut, that makes thee answer 'ay'.
If he be slain, say 'ay', or if not, 'no':
Brief sounds determine my weal or woe.

NURSE I saw the wound, I saw it with mine eyes
(God save the mark!), here on his manly breast:
A piteous corse, a bloody piteous corse,
Pale, pale as ashes, all bedaubed in blood,
All in gore blood — I sounded at the sight.

JULIET O break, my heart, poor bankrupt, break at once!
To prison, eyes, ne'er look on liberty!
Vile earth, to earth resign, end motion here,
And thou and Romeo press one heavy bier!

NURSE O Tybalt, Tybalt, the best friend I had!
O courteous Tybalt, honest gentleman,
That ever I should live to see thee dead!

JULIET What storm is this that blows so contrary?
Is Romeo slaughtered? And is Tybalt dead?
My dearest cousin, and my dearer lord?
Then, dreadful trumpet, sound the general doom,
For who is living, if those two are gone?

NURSE Tybalt is gone and Romeo banishèd.
Romeo that killed him, he is banishèd.

JULIET O God, did Romeo's hand shed Tybalt's blood?

NURSE It did, it did, alas the day, it did!

JULIET O serpent heart, hid with a flowering face!
Did ever dragon keep so fair a cave?
Beautiful tyrant, fiend angelical!
Dove-feathered raven, wolvish-ravening lamb!
Despisèd substance of divinest show!
Just opposite to what thou justly seem'st,
A damnèd saint, an honourable villain!
O nature, what hadst thou to do in hell
When thou didst bower the spirit of a fiend
In mortal paradise of such sweet flesh?
Was ever book containing such vile matter

Act 3, Scene 2

So fairly bound? O that deceit should dwell
In such a gorgeous palace!

NURSE
There's no trust,
No faith, no honesty in men, all perjured,
All forsworn, all naught, all dissemblers.
Ah, where's my man? Give me some aqua vitae.
These griefs, these woes, these sorrows make me old.
Shame come to Romeo!

JULIET
Blistered be thy tongue
For such a wish! He was not born to shame:
Upon his brow shame is ashamed to sit;
For 'tis a throne where honour may be crowned
Sole monarch of the universal earth.
O what a beast was I to chide at him!

NURSE
Will you speak well of him that killed your cousin?

JULIET
Shall I speak ill of him that is my husband?
Ah, poor my lord, what tongue shall smooth thy name,
When I, thy three-hours wife, have mangled it?
But wherefore, villain, didst thou kill my cousin?
That villain cousin would have killed my husband.
Back, foolish tears, back to your native spring,
Your tributary drops belong to woe,
Which you mistaking offer up to joy.
My husband lives that Tybalt would have slain,
And Tybalt's dead that would have slain my husband:
All this is comfort, wherefore weep I then?
Some word there was, worser than Tybalt's death,
That murdered me; I would forget it fain,
But O, it presses to my memory,
Like damnèd guilty deeds to sinners' minds:
'Tybalt is dead, and Romeo banishèd.'
That 'banishèd', that one word 'banishèd',
Hath slain ten thousand Tybalts. Tybalt's death
Was woe enough if it had ended there;
Or if sour woe delights in fellowship,
And needly will be ranked with other griefs,
Why followed not, when she said 'Tybalt's dead',
'Thy father' or 'thy mother', nay, or both,
Which modern lamentation might have moved?
But with a rear-ward following Tybalt's death,
'Romeo is banishèd': to speak that word,
Is father, mother, Tybalt, Romeo, Juliet,
All slain, all dead. 'Romeo is banishèd!'
There is no end, no limit, measure, bound,
In that word's death, no words can that woe sound.
Where is my father and my mother, Nurse?

NURSE
Weeping and wailing over Tybalt's corse.
Will you go to them? I will bring you thither.

JULIET
Wash they his wounds with tears? Mine shall be spent,
When theirs are dry, for Romeo's banishment.

88 'aqua vitae' means 'brandy.'

Character — Juliet

Juliet is angry when the Nurse curses Romeo. This shows that Juliet is loyal to him despite what he's done.

95 'chide' means 'be angry'.

Character — Juliet

Juliet is perceptive — she works out that Romeo was defending himself from Tybalt.

109 'fain' means 'gladly'.

113-114 In other words, 'hearing that Romeo is banished is ten thousand times worse than hearing that Tybalt is dead.'

120 'modern lamentation' means 'usual sadness'.

Theme — Family

Juliet feels as though Romeo's banishment is worse than the deaths of all her family combined. This shows that her love for Romeo is stronger than her love for her family.

129 'I will take you there'.

Act 3, Scene 3 — Romeo Hears He's Been Banished

132 'beguiled' means 'cheated'.

Shakespeare's Techniques

Juliet says that she will be married to death — this is a recurring image throughout the play.

138 'Go to your bedroom.'

139 'wot' means 'know'.

Take up those cords. Poor ropes, you are beguiled,
Both you and I, for Romeo is exiled.
He made you for a highway to my bed,
But I, a maid, die maiden-widowèd.
Come, cords, come, Nurse, I'll to my wedding bed,
And death, not Romeo, take my maidenhead!

NURSE Hie to your chamber. I'll find Romeo
To comfort you, I wot well where he is.
Hark ye, your Romeo will be here at night.
I'll to him, he is hid at Lawrence' cell.

JULIET O find him! Give this ring to my true knight,
And bid him come to take his last farewell.

Exeunt

Friar Lawrence tells Romeo that he's been banished. Romeo's upset but the Friar calms him down. The Nurse tells Romeo that Juliet is waiting for him in her bedroom and she gives him a ring from Juliet. Romeo heads off to say goodbye to Juliet.

ACT 3, SCENE 3

Shakespeare's Techniques

The Friar tells Romeo that he's married to misfortune. This is similar to Act 3, Scene 2 (lines 136-137). It reminds the audience that the couple can't escape their fate.

4 'doom' means 'judgement'.

5 In other words — 'What trouble is waiting for me?'

6-7 'You're too familiar with suffering.'

9 'Does the Prince want me dead?'

21 'mistermed' means 'wrongly named'.

FRIAR LAWRENCE'S CELL

Enter FRIAR LAWRENCE

FRIAR LAWRENCE Romeo, come forth; come forth, thou fearful man:
Affliction is enamoured of thy parts,
And thou art wedded to calamity.

Enter ROMEO

ROMEO Father, what news? What is the Prince's doom?
What sorrow craves acquaintance at my hand,
That I yet know not?

FRIAR LAWRENCE Too familiar
Is my dear son with such sour company.
I bring thee tidings of the Prince's doom.

ROMEO What less than doomsday is the Prince's doom?

FRIAR LAWRENCE A gentler judgement vanished from his lips,
Not body's death, but body's banishment.

ROMEO Ha, banishment! Be merciful, say 'death',
For exile hath more terror in his look,
Much more than death. Do not say 'banishment'.

FRIAR LAWRENCE Hence from Verona art thou banishèd:
Be patient, for the world is broad and wide.

ROMEO There is no world without Verona walls,
But purgatory, torture, hell itself.
Hence 'banishèd' is banished from the world,
And world's exile is death: then 'banishèd',
Is death mistermed. Calling death 'banishèd',
Thou cut'st my head off with a golden axe,
And smilest upon the stroke that murders me.

Act 3, Scene 3

FRIAR LAWRENCE O deadly sin! O rude unthankfulness!
Thy fault our law calls death, but the kind Prince,
Taking thy part, hath rushed aside the law,
And turned that black word 'death' to 'banishment'.
This is dear mercy, and thou seest it not.

ROMEO 'Tis torture, and not mercy: heaven is here,
Where Juliet lives, and every cat and dog
And little mouse, every unworthy thing,
Live here in heaven and may look on her,
But Romeo may not. More validity,
More honourable state, more courtship lives
In carrion flies than Romeo, they may seize
On the white wonder of dear Juliet's hand
And steal immortal blessing from her lips,
Who even in pure and vestal modesty,
Still blush, as thinking their own kisses sin.
But Romeo may not, he is banishèd.
Flies may do this, but I from this must fly:
They are free men, but I am banishèd.
And say'st thou yet that exile is not death?
Hadst thou no poison mixed, no sharp-ground knife,
No sudden mean of death, though ne'er so mean,
But 'banishèd' to kill me? 'Banishèd'?
O Friar, the damnèd use that word in hell;
Howling attends it. How hast thou the heart,
Being a divine, a ghostly confessor,
A sin-absolver, and my friend professed,
To mangle me with that word 'banishèd'?

FRIAR LAWRENCE Thou fond madman, hear me a little speak.

ROMEO O, thou wilt speak again of banishment.

FRIAR LAWRENCE I'll give thee armour to keep off that word:
Adversity's sweet milk, philosophy,
To comfort thee, though thou art banishèd.

ROMEO Yet 'banishèd'? Hang up philosophy!
Unless philosophy can make a Juliet,
Displant a town, reverse a prince's doom,
It helps not, it prevails not: talk no more.

FRIAR LAWRENCE O, then I see that madmen have no ears.

ROMEO How should they, when that wise men have no eyes?

FRIAR LAWRENCE Let me dispute with thee of thy estate.

ROMEO Thou canst not speak of that thou dost not feel:
Wert thou as young as I, Juliet thy love,
An hour but married, Tybalt murderèd,
Doting like me and like me banishèd,
Then mightst thou speak, then mightst thou tear thy hair,
And fall upon the ground, as I do now,
Taking the measure of an unmade grave.

Knocking within

FRIAR LAWRENCE Arise, one knocks. Good Romeo, hide thyself.

25-27 'By law, you should have been executed for what you did, but the Prince bent the rules for you'.

33 'validity' means 'value'.

35 'carrion flies' are flies that feed on rotting meat.

38 'vestal' means 'virginal'.

Shakespeare's Techniques

Romeo keeps repeating the word 'banished' — this shows his shock at the news.

45 'sudden mean' means 'quick method'.

50 'friend professed' means 'so-called friend'.

52 'fond' means 'foolish'.

Character — Romeo

Romeo childishly lashes out at Friar Lawrence. Romeo suggests that because Friar Lawrence can't marry, he can't really understand what Romeo is going through.

Act 3, Scene 3

74 'Hark' means 'listen'.

75 'You'll be caught.'

77 'simpleness' means 'stupidity'.

85 'He's in the same state as Juliet.'

91 'O' means 'moan'.

96-97 'now I have ruined our first moments as a married couple by killing her relative.'

99 'concealed lady' means 'secret wife'.

ROMEO Not I, unless the breath of heartsick groans,
Mist-like, infold me from the search of eyes.

Knock

FRIAR LAWRENCE Hark, how they knock! Who's there? Romeo,
arise! Thou wilt be taken. — Stay awhile! — Stand up;
Run to my study. — By and by! — God's will,
What simpleness is this? — I come, I come!

Knock

Who knocks so hard? Whence come you? What's your will?

NURSE (*Within*) Let me come in, and you shall know my errand;
I come from Lady Juliet.

FRIAR LAWRENCE Welcome, then. (*Unlocking door*)

Enter NURSE

NURSE O holy Friar, O, tell me, holy Friar,
Where is my lady's lord, where's Romeo?

FRIAR LAWRENCE There on the ground, with his own tears
made drunk.

NURSE O, he is even in my mistress' case,
Just in her case! O woeful sympathy!
Piteous predicament! Even so lies she,
Blubbering and weeping, weeping and blubbering.
Stand up, stand up. Stand, and you be a man:
For Juliet's sake, for her sake, rise and stand;
Why should you fall into so deep an O?

ROMEO Nurse!

He rises

NURSE Ah sir, ah sir, death's the end of all.

ROMEO Spakest thou of Juliet? How is it with her?
Doth not she think me an old murderer,
Now I have stained the childhood of our joy
With blood removed but little from her own?
Where is she? And how doth she? And what says
My concealed lady to our cancelled love?

NURSE O, she says nothing, sir, but weeps and weeps,
And now falls on her bed; and then starts up,
And Tybalt calls, and then on Romeo cries,
And then down falls again.

ROMEO As if that name,
Shot from the deadly level of a gun,
Did murder her — as that name's cursèd hand
Murdered her kinsman. O, tell me, Friar, tell me,
In what vile part of this anatomy
Doth my name lodge? Tell me, that I may sack
The hateful mansion.

Drawing his dagger

FRIAR LAWRENCE Hold thy desperate hand!
Art thou a man? Thy form cries out thou art:
Thy tears are womanish; thy wild acts denote

Character — Romeo

Romeo threatens to kill himself. This shows how impulsive he can be. He's also reckless — he doesn't consider the effect his suicide would have on Juliet.

Act 3, Scene 3

The unreasonable fury of a beast.
Unseemly woman in a seeming man,
Or ill-beseeming beast in seeming both!
Thou hast amazed me. By my holy order,
I thought thy disposition better tempered.
Hast thou slain Tybalt? Wilt thou slay thyself?
And slay thy lady that in thy life lives,
By doing damnèd hate upon thyself?
Why rail'st thou on thy birth, the heaven, and earth?
Since birth, and heaven, and earth, all three do meet
In thee at once; which thou at once wouldst lose.
Fie, fie, thou sham'st thy shape, thy love, thy wit.
Which, like a usurer, abound'st in all,
And usest none in that true use indeed
Which should bedeck thy shape, thy love, thy wit:
Thy noble shape is but a form of wax,
Digressing from the valour of a man;
Thy dear love sworn but hollow perjury,
Killing that love which thou hast vowed to cherish;
Thy wit, that ornament to shape and love,
Misshapen in the conduct of them both,
Like powder in a skilless soldier's flask,
Is set afire by thine own ignorance,
And thou dismembered with thine own defence.
What, rouse thee, man! Thy Juliet is alive,
For whose dear sake thou wast but lately dead;
There art thou happy. Tybalt would kill thee,
But thou slew'st Tybalt — there art thou happy.
The law that threatened death becomes thy friend,
And turns it to exile; there art thou happy:
A pack of blessings light upon thy back.
Happiness courts thee in her best array,
But, like a misbehavèd and sullen wench,
Thou pout'st upon thy fortune and thy love:
Take heed, take heed, for such die miserable.
Go, get thee to thy love, as was decreed,
Ascend her chamber, hence and comfort her:
But look thou stay not till the watch be set,
For then thou canst not pass to Mantua,
Where thou shalt live, till we can find a time
To blaze your marriage, reconcile your friends,
Beg pardon of the Prince, and call thee back
With twenty hundred thousand times more joy
Than thou went'st forth in lamentation.
Go before, Nurse: commend me to thy lady;
And bid her hasten all the house to bed,
Which heavy sorrow makes them apt unto.
Romeo is coming.

NURSE O Lord, I could have stayed here all the night
To hear good counsel. O, what learning is!
My lord, I'll tell my lady you will come.

Character — Friar Lawrence

Friar Lawrence stops Romeo from killing himself by telling him off. The Friar is angry at Romeo's irrational behaviour.

120 'rail'st' means 'rant'.

123 'You shame your good looks, your love, your intelligence.'

124 'usurer' means 'money lender'.

127 'form of wax' means 'waxwork figure' — Romeo lacks courage, so he's no longer a man.

133-135 'Your intelligence is like gunpowder in an untrained soldier's powder-flask — set alight by your own stupidity, blowing you to bits.'

Character — Friar Lawrence

Friar Lawrence is the voice of reason — he's reminding Romeo that banishment is a better sentence than death.

143 'array' means 'clothing'.

144-145 'You pout at your good luck like a sulky girl.'

149 'city guards are on duty'.

152 'blaze' means 'publicly announce'.

Act 3, Scene 4 — Capulet Agrees to Paris's Proposal

163 'Tell Juliet to get ready to be angry with me.'

167-169 'Go now — goodbye. Your whole future depends on this. Either leave before the guards are on duty, or at daybreak in disguise.'

170 'sojourn' means 'stay temporarily'.

Character — Romeo

Romeo's mood has changed dramatically — he's now excited about seeing Juliet. It suggests that Romeo's behaviour can be erratic.

ROMEO Do so, and bid my sweet prepare to chide.

NURSE offers to go in, and turns again

NURSE Here, sir, a ring she bid me give you, sir.
Hie you, make haste, for it grows very late.

Exit

ROMEO How well my comfort is revived by this!

FRIAR LAWRENCE Go hence; good night; and here stands all your state:
Either be gone before the watch be set,
Or by the break of day disguised from hence:
Sojourn in Mantua; I'll find out your man,
And he shall signify from time to time
Every good hap to you that chances here.
Give me thy hand, 'tis late. Farewell, good night.

ROMEO But that a joy past joy calls out on me,
It were a grief, so brief to part with thee:
Farewell.

Exeunt

Paris wants to court Juliet, but Capulet tells Paris she's too upset about Tybalt's death to see him. However, Capulet decides to let Paris marry Juliet on Thursday, and he sends Lady Capulet to tell Juliet his decision.

can be played as a comedy for light relief.

it can also be played seriously

ACT 3, SCENE 4

A ROOM IN CAPULET'S HOUSE

Enter CAPULET, LADY CAPULET *and* PARIS

2 'move' means 'convince'.

7 'abed' means 'in bed'.

8 'It's not right to court her in such sad times.'

11 'mewed up' means 'locked up'.

Theme — Family

Capulet thinks that Juliet will do as he says because she is "ruled / In all respects by me". This is ironic — Capulet doesn't know that Juliet has secretly married Romeo.

she has already disobeyed her father

CAPULET Things have fallen out, sir, so unluckily
That we have had no time to move our daughter.
Look you, she loved her kinsman Tybalt dearly,
And so did I. Well, we were born to die.
'Tis very late, she'll not come down tonight:
I promise you, but for your company,
I would have been abed an hour ago.

PARIS These times of woe afford no time to woo.
Madam, good night. Commend me to your daughter.

LADY CAPULET I will, and know her mind early tomorrow;
Tonight she is mewed up to her heaviness.

CAPULET Sir Paris, I will make a desperate tender
Of my child's love: I think she will be ruled
In all respects by me; nay, more, I doubt it not.
Wife, go you to her ere you go to bed,
Acquaint her here of my son Paris' love;
And bid her — mark you me — on Wednesday next —
But, soft, what day is this?

PARIS Monday, my lord,

it is now a forced marriage.

Act 3, Scene 5 — Juliet Refuses to Marry Paris

CAPULET
Monday, ha, ha! Well, Wednesday is too soon,
A'Thursday let it be: a'Thursday, tell her,
She shall be married to this noble earl.
Will you be ready? Do you like this haste?
We'll keep no great ado — a friend or two;
For, hark you, Tybalt being slain so late,
It may be thought we held him carelessly,
Being our kinsman, if we revel much:
Therefore we'll have some half a dozen friends,
And there an end. But what say you to Thursday?

PARIS
My lord, I would that Thursday were tomorrow.

CAPULET
Well, get you gone. A'Thursday be it then.
Go you to Juliet ere you go to bed,
Prepare her, wife, against this wedding day.
Farewell, my lord. Light to my chamber, ho!
Afore me, it is so very late that we
May call it early by and by. Good night.

Exeunt

Character — Capulet

Capulet agrees to Paris and Juliet's engagement. This contrasts with his attitude at the start of the play when he said that Juliet was too young to be married.

22-26 'Do you approve of this speediness? It won't be a big event, just a couple of friends — it might seem disrespectful to Tybalt if we have too big a party.'

Shakespeare's Techniques

This is a short scene — it emphasises how rushed Juliet's engagement is.

Romeo is in Juliet's room, but he has to leave because it's morning. Juliet pretends to Lady Capulet that she's upset because of Tybalt's death and that she hates Romeo. Lady Capulet tells Juliet that she is to marry Paris. Juliet refuses and has an argument with Capulet.

ACT 3, SCENE 5

JULIET'S BEDROOM

Enter ROMEO *and* JULIET *aloft at the window*

JULIET
Wilt thou be gone? It is not yet near day:
It was the nightingale, and not the lark,
That pierced the fearful hollow of thine ear;
Nightly she sings on yond pomegranate tree.
Believe me, love, it was the nightingale.

ROMEO
It was the lark, the herald of the morn,
No nightingale. Look, love, what envious streaks
Do lace the severing clouds in yonder east:
Night's candles are burnt out, and jocund day
Stands tiptoe on the misty mountain tops.
I must be gone and live, or stay and die.

JULIET
Yond light is not daylight, I know it, I:
It is some meteor that the sun exhaled
To be to thee this night a torch-bearer,
And light thee on thy way to Mantua.
Therefore stay yet, thou need'st not to be gone.

ROMEO
Let me be tane, let me be put to death,
I am content, so thou wilt have it so.
I'll say yon grey is not the morning's eye,
'Tis but the pale reflex of Cynthia's brow;
Nor that is not the lark whose notes do beat

2 Nightingales sing in the evening and larks sing in the morning — Juliet is pretending it's still evening.

9 'jocund' means 'joyful'.

17 'tane' means 'captured'.

20 'the moonlight' — 'Cynthia' is one name for the goddess of the moon.

Act 3, Scene 5

The vaulty heaven so high above our heads.
I have more care to stay than will to go:
Come, death, and welcome! Juliet wills it so.
How is't, my soul? Let's talk, it is not day.

JULIET
It is, it is, hie hence, be gone, away!
It is the lark that sings so out of tune,
Straining harsh discords and unpleasing sharps.
Some say the lark makes sweet division:
This doth not so, for she divideth us.
Some say the lark and loathèd toad changed eyes;
O now I would they had changed voices too,
Since arm from arm that voice doth us affray,
Hunting thee hence with hunt's-up to the day.
O now be gone, more light and light it grows.

ROMEO
More light and light, more dark and dark our woes!

Enter NURSE (*hastily*)

NURSE
Madam!

JULIET
Nurse?

NURSE
Your lady mother is coming to your chamber.
The day is broke, be wary, look about.

Exit

JULIET
Then, window, let day in, and let life out.

ROMEO
Farewell, farewell! One kiss, and I'll descend.

He goes down

JULIET
Art thou gone so, love, lord, ay husband, friend?
I must hear from thee every day in the hour,
For in a minute there are many days.
O, by this count I shall be much in years
Ere I again behold my Romeo!

ROMEO
(*From below*) Farewell!
I will omit no opportunity
That may convey my greetings, love, to thee.

JULIET
O think'st thou we shall ever meet again?

ROMEO
I doubt it not, and all these woes shall serve
For sweet discourses in our times to come.

JULIET
O God, I have an ill-divining soul!
Methinks I see thee now, thou art so low,
As one dead in the bottom of a tomb.
Either my eyesight fails, or thou look'st pale.

ROMEO
And trust me, love, in my eye so do you:
Dry sorrow drinks our blood. Adieu, adieu!

Exit

JULIET
O Fortune, Fortune, all men call thee fickle;
If thou art fickle, what dost thou with him
That is renowned for faith? Be fickle, Fortune:
For then I hope thou wilt not keep him long,
But send him back.

Enter LADY CAPULET *below*

---

29 'division' means 'complicated melody' or 'separation'.

33 'affray' means 'frighten'.

34 'hunt's-up' is a song played to wake up hunters early in the morning.

41 By 'life' she means Romeo.

45-47 In other words — 'Every minute will seem like days. By that reckoning I'll be much older when I see you again.'

54 'I have a bad feeling about this.'

Shakespeare's Techniques

Juliet has a vision of Romeo dead at the bottom of a tomb. This foreshadows the next time Juliet will see Romeo — he will be dead in the Capulet tomb.

Act 3, Scene 5

LADY CAPULET Ho, daughter, are you up?

JULIET Who is't that calls? It is my lady mother.
Is she not down so late, or up so early?
What unaccustomed cause procures her hither?

She goes down from the window and enters below

LADY CAPULET Why how now, Juliet?

JULIET Madam, I am not well.

LADY CAPULET Evermore weeping for your cousin's death?
What, wilt thou wash him from his grave with tears?
And if thou couldst, thou couldst not make him live;
Therefore have done. Some grief shows much of love,
But much of grief shows still some want of wit.

JULIET Yet let me weep for such a feeling loss.

LADY CAPULET So shall you feel the loss, but not the friend
Which you weep for.

JULIET Feeling so the loss,
I cannot choose but ever weep the friend.

LADY CAPULET Well, girl, thou weep'st not so much for his death
As that the villain lives which slaughtered him.

JULIET What villain, madam?

LADY CAPULET That same villain Romeo,

JULIET (*Aside*) Villain and he be many miles asunder —
God pardon him, I do with all my heart:
And yet no man like he doth grieve my heart.

LADY CAPULET That is because the traitor murderer lives.

JULIET Ay, madam, from the reach of these my hands.
Would none but I might venge my cousin's death!

LADY CAPULET We will have vengeance for it, fear thou not:
Then weep no more. I'll send to one in Mantua,
Where that same banished runagate doth live,
Shall give him such an unaccustomed dram
That he shall soon keep Tybalt company;
And then I hope thou wilt be satisfied.

JULIET Indeed I never shall be satisfied
With Romeo, till I behold him — dead —
Is my poor heart, so for a kinsman vexed.
Madam, if you could find out but a man
To bear a poison, I would temper it,
That Romeo should upon receipt thereof
Soon sleep in quiet. O how my heart abhors
To hear him named and cannot come to him,
To wreak the love I bore my cousin
Upon his body that hath slaughtered him!

LADY CAPULET Find thou the means, and I'll find such a man
But now I'll tell thee joyful tidings, girl.

JULIET And joy comes well in such a needy time.
What are they, I beseech your ladyship?

LADY CAPULET Well, well, thou hast a careful father, child,

full of care; taker care of her

66-67 'Has she not gone to bed, or has she got up really early? What unusual reason brings her here?'

69-70 Lady Capulet thinks that Juliet's upset over Tybalt.

Character — Lady Capulet

Lady Capulet is unsympathetic even though Juliet is upset. She thinks Juliet's sadness is over the top.

81 'asunder' means 'apart'.

83 Juliet says that no one hurts her heart as much as Romeo does, but she pretends that's because he killed Tybalt.

Shakespeare's Techniques

Lady Capulet threatens to poison Romeo because she hates him. This foreshadows Romeo poisoning himself in the final scene out of love for Juliet.

89 'runagate' means 'scoundrel' (she means Romeo).

90 'unaccustomed dram' means 'poison'.

Shakespeare's Techniques

Juliet is pretending that she hates Romeo. She uses words with double meanings so that she says the opposite of what her mother thinks she's saying.

97 'temper' means 'mix' or 'weaken'.

99 'abhors' means 'hates'.

101 'wreak' means 'inflict'.

106 'may I ask?'

Act 3, Scene 5

One who, to put thee from thy heaviness,
Hath sorted out a sudden day of joy,
That thou expects not, nor I looked not for.

JULIET Madam, in happy time, what day is that?

LADY CAPULET Marry, my child, early next Thursday morn,
The gallant, young, and noble gentleman,
The County Paris, at Saint Peter's Church,
Shall happily make thee there a joyful bride.

JULIET Now by Saint Peter's Church and Peter too,
He shall not make me there a joyful bride.
I wonder at this haste, that I must wed
Ere he that should be husband comes to woo.
I pray you tell my lord and father, madam,
I will not marry yet, and when I do, I swear
It shall be Romeo, whom you know I hate,
Rather than Paris. These are news indeed!

118-119 'Why the rush for me to marry him when we barely know each other?'

LADY CAPULET Here comes your father, tell him so yourself;
And see how he will take it at your hands.

125 'See how he reacts when you tell him.'

Enter CAPULET *and* NURSE

CAPULET When the sun sets, the earth doth drizzle dew,
But for the sunset of my brother's son
It rains downright.
How now, a conduit, girl? What, still in tears?
Evermore showering? In one little body
Thou counterfeits a bark, a sea, a wind:
For still thy eyes, which I may call the sea,
Do ebb and flow with tears; the bark thy body is,
Sailing in this salt flood; the winds thy sighs,
Who, raging with thy tears and they with them,
Without a sudden calm, will overset
Thy tempest-tossèd body. How now, wife,
Have you delivered to her our decree?

127 By 'sunset' he means 'death'.

129 'conduit' means 'fountain'.

131 'counterfeits a bark' means 'resemble a boat'.

LADY CAPULET Ay, sir, but she will none, she gives you thanks.
I would the fool were married to her grave.

CAPULET Soft, take me with you, take me with you, wife.
How, will she none? Doth she not give us thanks?
Is she not proud? Doth she not count her blest,
Unworthy as she is, that we have wrought
So worthy a gentleman to be her bride?

141 'Explain what you mean.'

Character — Capulet

Capulet's repeated questions show how shocked and angry he is. He can't believe that his daughter would defy him.

JULIET Not proud you have, but thankful that you have:
Proud can I never be of what I hate,
But thankful even for hate that is meant love.

CAPULET How how, how how, chopt-logic? What is this?
'Proud', and 'I thank you', and 'I thank you not',
And yet 'not proud', mistress minion you?
Thank me no thankings, nor proud me no prouds,
But fettle your fine joints 'gainst Thursday next,
To go with Paris to Saint Peter's Church,
Or I will drag thee on a hurdle thither.
Out, you green-sickness carrion! Out, you baggage!

149 'chopt-logic' means 'someone who twists words'.

153 'get yourself ready'

155 A 'hurdle' is a sledge on which people were dragged to their execution.

Act 3, Scene 5

You tallow-face!

LADY CAPULET Fie, fie, what, are you mad?

JULIET Good father, I beseech you on my knees,
Hear me with patience but to speak a word.

She kneels down

CAPULET Hang thee, young baggage, disobedient wretch!
I tell thee what: get thee to church a'Thursday,
Or never after look me in the face.
Speak not, reply not, do not answer me!
My fingers itch. Wife, we scarce thought us blest
That God had lent us but this only child,
But now I see this one is one too much,
And that we have a curse in having her.
Out on her, hilding!

NURSE God in heaven bless her!
You are to blame, my lord, to rate her so.

CAPULET And why, my Lady Wisdom? Hold your tongue,
Good Prudence, smatter with your gossips, go.

NURSE I speak no treason.

CAPULET O God-i-goden!

NURSE May not one speak?

CAPULET Peace, you mumbling fool!
Utter your gravity o'er a gossip's bowl,
For here we need it not.

LADY CAPULET You are too hot.

CAPULET God's bread, it makes me mad! Day, night, work, play,
Alone, in company, still my care hath been
To have her matched; and having now provided
A gentleman of noble parentage,
Of fair demesnes, youthful and nobly ligned,
Stuffed, as they say, with honourable parts,
Proportioned as one's thought would wish a man,
And then to have a wretched puling fool,
A whining mammet, in her fortune's tender,
To answer 'I'll not wed, I cannot love
I am too young, I pray you pardon me.'
But and you will not wed, I'll pardon you:
Graze where you will, you shall not house with me.
Look to't, think on't, I do not use to jest.
Thursday is near, lay hand on heart, advise:
And you be mine, I'll give you to my friend;
And you be not, hang, beg, starve, die in the streets,
For by my soul, I'll ne'er acknowledge thee,
Nor what is mine shall never do thee good.
Trust to't, bethink you, I'll not be forsworn.

Exit

JULIET Is there no pity sitting in the clouds
That sees into the bottom of my grief?
O sweet my mother, cast me not away!

157 'tallow-face' means 'pale face'.

Character — Juliet

Juliet is on her knees begging her father — it's a powerful scene and this shows how desperate she is.

Character — Capulet

Capulet's anger at Juliet's disobedience shows how controlling he is — he's used to getting his own way. Capulet's lack of sympathy helps the audience relate to Juliet's unhappiness.

169 'rate' means 'tell off'.

171 'Go and natter with your cronies'.

172 'O God-i-goden' means 'good evening' (get out).

174-175 'Save your advice for your cronies. We don't need it here.'

180 'ligned' means 'descended' — he belongs to a noble family.

183 'puling' means 'crying'.

184 'mammet' means 'puppet'.

191-192 In other words — 'If you're my obedient daughter, I'll marry you to Paris, and if you're not...'

Act 3, Scene 5

Delay this marriage for a month, a week,
Or if you do not, make the bridal bed
In that dim monument where Tybalt lies.

203 'Do what you want, I am finished with you.'

LADY CAPULET Talk not to me, for I'll not speak a word.
Do as thou wilt, for I have done with thee.

Exit

Theme — Religion

If Juliet is forced to marry Paris, she'd be committing a terrible sin — she's already married to Romeo.

JULIET O God! — O Nurse, how shall this be prevented?
My husband is on earth, my faith in heaven;
How shall that faith return again to earth,
Unless that husband send it me from heaven
By leaving earth? Comfort me, counsel me.
Alack, alack, that heaven should practise stratagems
Upon so soft a subject as myself!
What say'st thou? Hast thou not a word of joy?
Some comfort, Nurse.

Character — The Nurse

The Nurse tells Juliet to forget Romeo and marry Paris instead — she doesn't understand how much Juliet loves Romeo, or seem to care that it's a sin. Juliet doesn't confide in the Nurse after this scene — Juliet lies to her in lines 230-233.

NURSE Faith, here it is:
Romeo is banished, and all the world to nothing
That he dares ne'er come back to challenge you;
Or if he do, it needs must be by stealth.
Then since the case so stands as now it doth,
I think it best you married with the County.
O, he's a lovely gentleman!
Romeo's a dishclout to him. An eagle, madam,
Hath not so green, so quick, so fair an eye
As Paris hath. Beshrew my very heart,
I think you are happy in this second match,
For it excels your first, or if it did not,
Your first is dead, or 'twere as good he were
As living here and you no use of him.

219 'dishclout' means 'dishcloth'.

221 'beshrew' means 'curse'.

JULIET Speak'st thou from thy heart?

NURSE And from my soul too, else beshrew them both.

JULIET Amen.

NURSE What?

JULIET Well, thou hast comforted me marvellous much.
Go in, and tell my lady I am gone,
Having displeased my father, to Lawrence' cell,
To make confession and to be absolved.

234 'Indeed I will — it's a good idea.'

NURSE Marry, I will, and this is wisely done.

Exit

236 'to want me to break my marriage vows'.

JULIET (*She looks after Nurse*)
Ancient damnation! O most wicked fiend!
Is it more sin to wish me thus forsworn,
Or to dispraise my lord with that same tongue
Which she hath praised him with above compare
So many thousand times? Go, counsellor,
Thou and my bosom henceforth shall be twain.
I'll to the Friar to know his remedy;
If all else fail, myself have power to die.

Exit

Shakespeare's Techniques

At the end of the scene, Juliet is alone on the stage. This is symbolic — she has been separated from her family and can't turn to them for help. This shows how desperate she is and explains why she is so eager to agree to the fake suicide in the next scene.

Act Three — Practice Questions

Quick Questions

1) How does Romeo react to Tybalt's challenge at first?
2) What is Romeo's punishment for killing Tybalt?
3) What does the Nurse promise to do at the end of Act 3, Scene 2?
4) Why does Friar Lawrence think Romeo is lucky to be banished in Act 3, Scene 3?
5) What is Friar Lawrence's plan at the end of Act 3, Scene 3?
6) In Act 3, Scene 4, when does Capulet want the wedding to take place?
7) How does Romeo escape from Juliet's room in Act 3, Scene 5?
8) What does Lady Capulet think Juliet is crying about?
9) How does Juliet react to being told that she is to marry Paris?
10) What does Juliet mean when she says "If all else fail, myself have power to die"?

In-depth Questions

1) Why do you think Mercutio tries to provoke Tybalt into a fight? Explain your answer.
2) Do you think that the violence in Act 3, Scene 1 was inevitable?
3) Do you think Romeo's reaction to his banishment in Act 3, Scene 3 is understandable or excessive? Explain your choice.
4) Why do you think Shakespeare has Tybalt stab Mercutio under Romeo's arm?
5) Why do you think Capulet agrees to Juliet and Paris's engagement?
6) Do you think the Nurse has Juliet's best interests at heart when she tells Juliet that she should forget about Romeo and marry Paris? Give reasons for your answer.
7) Write a diary entry from Juliet's point of view explaining how she feels about her engagement to Paris. Include how she feels about her parents and the Nurse.

Act 4, Scene 1 — Friar Lawrence has a Plan

Paris, Friar Lawrence and Juliet are at Friar Lawrence's cell. Paris tries to flirt with Juliet, but she refuses to play along. Paris leaves and Juliet tells the Friar that she'd rather kill herself than marry Paris. Friar Lawrence has a plan — he gives Juliet a potion to drink that evening which will make her look dead.

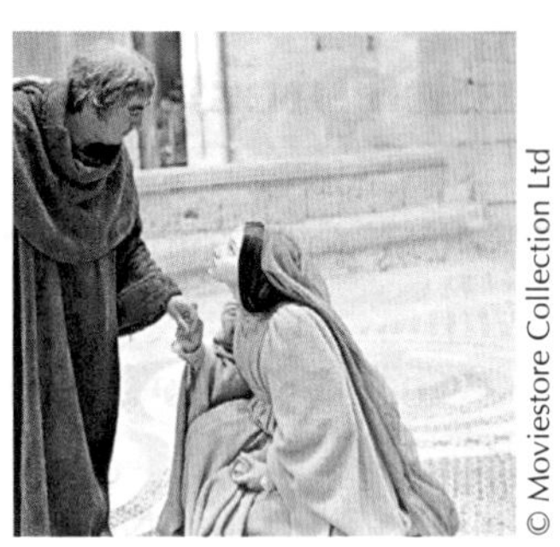

© Moviestore Collection Ltd

ACT 4, SCENE 1

FRIAR LAWRENCE'S CELL

Enter FRIAR LAWRENCE *and* PARIS

FRIAR LAWRENCE On Thursday, sir? The time is very short.

PARIS My father Capulet will have it so,
And I am nothing slow to slack his haste.

FRIAR LAWRENCE You say you do not know the lady's mind?
Uneven is the course, I like it not.

PARIS Immoderately she weeps for Tybalt's death,
And therefore have I little talked of love,
For Venus smiles not in a house of tears.
Now, sir, her father counts it dangerous
That she do give her sorrow so much sway,
And in his wisdom hastes our marriage
To stop the inundation of her tears,
Which too much minded by herself alone
May be put from her by society.
Now do you know the reason of this haste.

FRIAR LAWRENCE (*Aside*) I would I knew not why it should be slowed.
Look, sir, here comes the lady toward my cell.

Enter JULIET

PARIS Happily met, my lady and my wife!

JULIET That may be, sir, when I may be a wife.

PARIS That 'may be' must be, love, on Thursday next.

JULIET What must be shall be.

FRIAR LAWRENCE That's a certain text.

PARIS Come you to make confession to this father?

JULIET To answer that, I should confess to you.

PARIS Do not deny to him that you love me.

JULIET I will confess to you that I love him.

PARIS So will ye, I am sure, that you love me.

JULIET If I do so, it will be of more price,
Being spoke behind your back, than to your face.

PARIS Poor soul, thy face is much abused with tears.

JULIET The tears have got small victory by that,
For it was bad enough before their spite.

PARIS Thou wrong'st it more than tears with that report.

JULIET That is no slander, sir, which is a truth,

3 'I'm eager too — I don't want to slow him down'.

9-12 Paris explains that Lord Capulet wants Juliet to be married, to take her mind off Tybalt's death, and that is the reason for the rush.

12 'inundation' means 'floods'.

16 'I wish I didn't know why the wedding should be delayed'.

Character — Juliet

Juliet is quite hostile when she's talking to Paris — she tries to appear polite, but she barely hides her true feelings. This adds to the tension of the scene.

Character — Juliet

Juliet manages to avoid giving Paris a straight answer — this shows her intelligence and ability to think quickly.

29 'Poor thing, your face is streaked with tears.'

30-31 'The tears haven't made my face look that much worse — I was ugly enough before I started crying'.

Act 4, Scene 1

And what I spake, I spake it to my face.

PARIS Thy face is mine, and thou hast slandered it.

JULIET It may be so, for it is not mine own.
Are you at leisure, holy father, now,
Or shall I come to you at evening mass?

FRIAR LAWRENCE My leisure serves me, pensive daughter, now.
My lord, we must entreat the time alone.

PARIS God shield I should disturb devotion!
Juliet, on Thursday early will I rouse ye;
Till then adieu, and keep this holy kiss.

Exit

JULIET O shut the door, and when thou hast done so,
Come weep with me, past hope, past cure, past help!

FRIAR LAWRENCE O Juliet, I already know thy grief,
It strains me past the compass of my wits.
I hear thou must, and nothing may prorogue it,
On Thursday next be married to this County.

JULIET Tell me not, Friar, that thou hearest of this,
Unless thou tell me how I may prevent it.
If in thy wisdom thou canst give no help,
Do thou but call my resolution wise,
And with this knife I'll help it presently.
God joined my heart and Romeo's, thou our hands,
And ere this hand, by thee to Romeo's sealed,
Shall be the label to another deed,
Or my true heart with treacherous revolt
Turn to another, this shall slay them both.
Therefore, out of thy long-experienced time,
Give me some present counsel, or, behold,
'Twixt my extremes and me this bloody knife
Shall play the umpire, arbitrating that
Which the commission of thy years and art
Could to no issue of true honour bring.
Be not so long to speak, I long to die,
If what thou speak'st speak not of remedy.

FRIAR LAWRENCE Hold, daughter, I do spy a kind of hope,
Which craves as desperate an execution
As that is desperate which we would prevent.
If, rather than to marry County Paris,
Thou hast the strength of will to slay thyself,
Then is it likely thou wilt undertake
A thing like death to chide away this shame,
That cop'st with Death himself to scape from it;
And if thou dar'st, I'll give thee remedy.

JULIET O bid me leap, rather than marry Paris,
From off the battlements of any tower,
Or walk in thievish ways, or bid me lurk
Where serpents are; chain me with roaring bears,
Or hide me nightly in a charnel-house,
O'ercovered quite with dead men's rattling bones,

37 'at leisure' means 'free' or 'available'.

39 'pensive' means 'worried'.

41 'God shield' means 'God forbid'.

42 'rouse ye' means 'wake you up'.

Character — Juliet

As soon as Paris leaves, Juliet's language becomes more dramatic, emphasising how emotional she is.

48 'prorogue' means 'postpone'.

Character — Friar Lawrence

The Friar feels partly responsible for the situation — he married the couple, so he can't let Juliet marry Paris.

56 'ere' means 'before'.

62-63 'Between my terrible problems and me, this knife will be the judge'.

Character — Juliet

Juliet is suicidal — this shows her desperation.

64 'commission' means 'authority'.

69-70 'which calls for drastic action, almost as desperate as what we're trying to stop'.

73-75 'You will go through something like death to chase away this shame, you will face death in order to escape it.'

76 'dar'st' means 'dare'.

81 'charnel-house' is a tomb where bones from old graves are kept.

Act 4, Scene 1

dramatic irony - the audience knows the plan won't work

Character — Juliet

Juliet's horrific language shows that she's afraid, but the fact that she's willing to do whatever it takes shows how much she loves Romeo.

83 'stinking leg bones and yellow jawless skulls'.

89 'give consent' means 'say yes'.

91 'look' means 'make sure'.

93 'vial' means 'small bottle'.

95-97 'a cold and tranquillising liquid will run through your veins, stopping your pulse.'

100 'wanny' means 'pale'.

110 'bier' means 'a frame used to carry a body to the grave'.

113 'while we wait for you to wake up'.

114 'drift' means 'plan'.

119-120 'as long as no second thoughts or fears stop you from doing it'.

Shakespeare's Techniques

Shakespeare uses rhyme to emphasise that Friar Lawrence and Juliet agree.

125 'strength will give me help'.

With reeky shanks and yellow chapless skulls;
Or bid me go into a new-made grave,
And hide me with a dead man in his shroud —
Things that to hear them told have made me tremble —
And I will do it without fear or doubt,
To live an unstained wife to my sweet love.

FRIAR LAWRENCE Hold then, go home, be merry, give consent
To marry Paris. Wednesday is tomorrow;
Tomorrow night look that thou lie alone,
Let not the Nurse lie with thee in thy chamber.
Take thou this vial, being then in bed,
And this distilling liquor drink thou off,
When presently through all thy veins shall run
A cold and drowsy humour, for no pulse
Shall keep his native progress, but surcease;
No warmth, no breath shall testify thou livest,
The roses in thy lips and cheeks shall fade
To wanny ashes, thy eyes' windows fall,
Like Death when he shuts up the day of life.
Each part, deprived of supple government,
Shall stiff and stark and cold appear like death,
And in this borrowed likeness of shrunk death
Thou shalt continue two and forty hours,
And then awake as from a pleasant sleep.
Now when the bridegroom in the morning comes
To rouse thee from thy bed, there art thou dead.
Then as the manner of our country is,
In thy best robes, uncovered on the bier,
Thou shall be borne to that same ancient vault
Where all the kindred of the Capulets lie.
In the mean time, against thou shalt awake,
Shall Romeo by my letters know our drift,
And hither shall he come, and he and I
Will watch thy waking, and that very night
Shall Romeo bear thee hence to Mantua.
And this shall free thee from this present shame,
If no inconstant toy, nor womanish fear,
Abate thy valour in the acting it.

JULIET Give me, give me! O tell me not of fear.

FRIAR LAWRENCE Hold, get you gone, be strong and prosperous
In this resolve. I'll send a friar with speed
To Mantua, with my letters to thy lord.

JULIET Love give me strength, and strength shall help afford.
Farewell, dear father.

Exeunt

The plan is deliberately risky to create uncertainty and suspense. This is like the folk tale "Sleeping Beauty" - this suggests that the plan is an unrealistic fairy tale.

Act 4, Scene 2 — The Wedding is Moved Forward

Juliet returns from Friar Lawrence's cell and pretends that she's happy to marry Paris. She asks for her father's forgiveness. Lord Capulet is so delighted he decides to have the wedding a day early.

ACT 4, SCENE 2

CAPULET'S MANSION

Enter CAPULET, LADY CAPULET, NURSE, *and two or three* SERVINGMEN

CAPULET So many guests invite as here are writ.

Exit SERVINGMAN

Sirrah, go hire me twenty cunning cooks.

SERVINGMAN You shall have none ill, sir, for I'll try if they can lick their fingers.

CAPULET How canst thou try them so?

SERVINGMAN Marry, sir, 'tis an ill cook that cannot lick his own fingers; therefore he that cannot lick his fingers goes not with me.

CAPULET Go, be gone.

Exit SERVINGMAN

We shall be much unfurnished for this time.
What, is my daughter gone to Friar Lawrence?

NURSE Ay forsooth.

CAPULET Well, he may chance to do some good on her.
A peevish self-willed harlotry it is.

Enter JULIET

NURSE See where she comes from shrift with merry look.

CAPULET How now, my headstrong, where have you been gadding?

JULIET Where I have learnt me to repent the sin
Of disobedient opposition
To you and your behests, and am enjoined
By holy Lawrence to fall prostrate here
To beg your pardon.

She kneels down

Pardon, I beseech you!
Henceforward I am ever ruled by you.

CAPULET Send for the County, go tell him of this.
I'll have this knot knit up tomorrow morning.

JULIET I met the youthful lord at Lawrence' cell,
And gave him what becomèd love I might,
Not stepping o'er the bounds of modesty.

CAPULET Why, I am glad on't, this is well, stand up.

Shakespeare's Techniques

This is a busy scene, which is full of activity in preparation for another party — it contrasts with Juliet's desperation in the scene before.

2 'cunning' means 'skilful'.

10 'unfurnished' means 'unprepared'.

12 'Ay forsooth' means 'yes indeed'.

15 'shrift' means 'confession'.

19 'behests' means 'orders'.

19 'enjoined' means 'told'.

Character — Juliet

Juliet fools her family into thinking she will marry Paris. She lies to make sure the Friar's plan goes ahead.

24 'I'll have this wedding take place tomorrow morning.'

25-27 'I met Paris at the Friar's cell. I was nice to him without being too forward.'

Act 4, Scene 3 — Juliet Takes the Potion

Shakespeare's Techniques

Capulet is praising Friar Lawrence. This is ironic — Friar Lawrence has secretly married Romeo and Juliet.

33-35 'Nurse, come to my room to help me sort out the things you think I'll need tomorrow'.

41 'get her dressed up'.

46 'Against tomorrow' means 'for tomorrow'.

Character — Capulet

Capulet's mood changes — he's happy and excited now he's got his own way.

This is as't should be. Let me see the County;
Ay, marry, go, I say, and fetch him hither.
Now afore God, this reverend holy Friar,
All our whole city is much bound to him.

JULIET Nurse, will you go with me into my closet,
To help me sort such needful ornaments
As you think fit to furnish me tomorrow?

LADY CAPULET No, not till Thursday, there is time enough.

CAPULET Go, Nurse, go with her, we'll to church tomorrow.

Exeunt JULIET *and* NURSE

LADY CAPULET We shall be short in our provision,
'Tis now near night.

CAPULET Tush, I will stir about,
And all things shall be well, I warrant thee, wife.
Go thou to Juliet, help to deck up her.
I'll not to bed tonight; let me alone,
I'll play the housewife for this once. What ho!
They are all forth. Well, I will walk myself
To County Paris, to prepare up him
Against tomorrow. My heart is wondrous light,
Since this same wayward girl is so reclaimed.

Exeunt

Juliet is alone in her room. She speaks her final big soliloquy — she's afraid to take the potion and doubts the Friar's motives. She imagines Romeo being hunted by a ghostly Tybalt and decides to drink the potion.

ACT 4, SCENE 3

1 'attires' means 'clothes'.

3 'orisons' means 'prayers'.

5 'cross' means 'unfavourable'.

7-8 'No mother, we've got all the things ready that we'll need tomorrow'.

JULIET'S BEDROOM

Enter JULIET *and* NURSE

JULIET Ay, those attires are best, but, gentle Nurse,
I pray thee leave me to myself tonight:
For I have need of many orisons
To move the heavens to smile upon my state,
Which, well thou knowest, is cross and full of sin.

Enter LADY CAPULET

LADY CAPULET What, are you busy, ho? Need you my help?

JULIET No, madam, we have culled such necessaries
As are behoveful for our state tomorrow.
So please you, let me now be left alone,
And let the Nurse this night sit up with you,
For I am sure you have your hands full all,
In this so sudden business.

LADY CAPULET Good night.
Get thee to bed and rest, for thou hast need.

Act 4, Scene 3

Exeunt LADY CAPULET *and* NURSE

JULIET Farewell! God knows when we shall meet again.
I have a faint cold fear thrills through my veins
That almost freezes up the heat of life.
I'll call them back again to comfort me.
Nurse! What should she do here?
My dismal scene I needs must act alone.
Come, vial.
What if this mixture do not work at all?
Shall I be married then tomorrow morning?
No, no, this shall forbid it; lie thou there.

Laying down her dagger

What if it be a poison which the Friar
Subtly hath ministered to have me dead,
Lest in this marriage he should be dishonoured,
Because he married me before to Romeo?
I fear it is, and yet methinks it should not,
For he hath still been tried a holy man.
How if, when I am laid into the tomb,
I wake before the time that Romeo
Come to redeem me? There's a fearful point!
Shall I not then be stifled in the vault,
To whose foul mouth no healthsome air breathes in,
And there die strangled ere my Romeo comes?
Or if I live, is it not very like
The horrible conceit of death and night,
Together with the terror of the place —
As in a vault, an ancient receptacle,
Where for this many hundred years the bones
Of all my buried ancestors are packed,
Where bloody Tybalt, yet but green in earth,
Lies festering in his shroud, where, as they say,
At some hours in the night spirits resort —
Alack, alack, is it not like that I,
So early waking — what with loathsome smells,
And shrieks like mandrakes torn out of the earth,
That living mortals hearing them run mad —
O, if I wake, shall I not be distraught,
Environèd with all these hideous fears,
And madly play with my forefathers' joints,
And pluck the mangled Tybalt from his shroud,
And in this rage, with some great kinsman's bone,
As with a club, dash out my desp'rate brains?
O look! Methinks I see my cousin's ghost
Seeking out Romeo that did spit his body
Upon a rapier's point. Stay, Tybalt, stay!
Romeo, Romeo, Romeo! Here's drink — I drink to thee.

She falls upon her bed, within the curtains

15 'A cold fear runs through my veins, making me feel faint'.

19 'In my desperation I must act alone.'

Shakespeare's Techniques

Juliet doubts Friar Lawrence. This shows her uncertainty and adds to the suspense of the scene.

29 'tried' means 'proved to be'.

Shakespeare's Techniques

Juliet worries that she'll wake up before Romeo arrives. This is ironic — Juliet wakes up too late to stop Romeo from killing himself.

Character — Juliet

Juliet's gruesome language reminds the audience that what she's going to do is really horrifying — lie in a sealed tomb with her cousin's rotting body.

47 'mandrakes' are a type of plant — it was thought that they screamed when you pulled them up.

50 'Environèd' means 'surrounded'.

Act 4, Scene 4 — The Wedding Preparations

The Capulet family are up late preparing everything for the wedding the following morning. Paris arrives and the Nurse is sent upstairs to wake Juliet.

ACT 4, SCENE 4

A ROOM IN CAPULET'S MANSION

Enter LADY CAPULET *and* NURSE *with herbs*

LADY CAPULET Hold, take these keys and fetch more spices, Nurse.

NURSE They call for dates and quinces in the pastry.

Enter CAPULET

CAPULET Come, stir, stir, stir! The second cock hath crowed,
The curfew bell hath rung, 'tis three a'clock.
Look to the baked meats, good Angelica,
Spare not for cost.

NURSE Go, you cot-quean, go,
Get you to bed. Faith, you'll be sick tomorrow
For this night's watching.

CAPULET No, not a whit. What, I have watched ere now
All night for lesser cause, and ne'er been sick.

LADY CAPULET Ay, you have been a mouse-hunt in your time,
But I will watch you from such watching now.

Exeunt LADY CAPULET *and* NURSE

CAPULET A jealous hood, a jealous hood!

Enter three or four SERVINGMEN *with spits and logs and baskets.*

Now, fellow,
What is there?

FIRST SERVINGMAN Things for the cook, sir, but I know not what.

CAPULET Make haste, make haste.

Exit FIRST SERVINGMAN

Sirrah, fetch drier logs.
Call Peter, he will show thee where they are.

SECOND SERVINGMAN I have a head, sir, that will find out logs,
And never trouble Peter for the matter.

CAPULET Mass, and well said, a merry whoreson, ha!
Thou shalt be loggerhead.

Exeunt SECOND SERVINGMAN *and any others*

Good faith, 'tis day.
The County will be here with music straight,
For so he said he would.

Music from within

I hear him near.
Nurse! Wife! What ho! What, Nurse, I say!

Enter NURSE

Go waken Juliet, go and trim her up,
I'll go and chat with Paris. Hie, make haste,
Make haste, the bridegroom he is come already,
Make haste, I say.

Exit

2 'pastry' means 'kitchen'.

6-8 'Go to bed you house-husband. You'll be ill tomorrow for lack of sleep.'

9-10 'No, not at all. I've been up all night for less important things and never been ill'.

11 'mouse-hunt' means 'chasing women'.

Character — Capulet

Lady Capulet teases her husband and Capulet jokes with the servingman. This upbeat scene is juxtaposed with the discovery of Juliet's body to increase the tension.

21 'loggerhead' means 'blockhead'.

21-22 'Goodness, it's daytime. Paris will be here any minute with the musicians'.

Shakespeare's Techniques

This scene echoes Act 1, Scene 5 when the Capulets were getting ready for the ball. Then the play was moving towards romance, but now it's headed towards tragedy.

dramatic irony throughout the scene

Act 4, Scene 5 — The Capulets find Juliet's Body

The Nurse discovers Juliet's body and the Capulets mourn their daughter's death. Friar Lawrence calms them down and they start organising the funeral.

ACT 4, SCENE 5

JULIET'S CHAMBER

Enter NURSE

NURSE
Mistress! What, mistress! Juliet! Fast, I warrant her, she.
Why, lamb! Why, lady! Fie, you slug-a-bed!
Why, love, I say! Madam! Sweetheart! Why, bride!
What, not a word? You take your pennyworths now,
Sleep for a week, for the next night I warrant,
The County Paris hath set up his rest,
That you shall rest but little. God forgive me,
Marry, and amen, how sound is she asleep!
I needs must wake her. Madam, madam, madam!
Ay, let the county take you in your bed,
He'll fright you up, i'faith. Will it not be?

Undraws the curtains

What, dressed! And in your clothes! And down again!
I must needs wake you. Lady! Lady! Lady!
Alas, alas! Help, help! My lady's dead!
O, well-a-day, that ever I was born!
Some aqua vitae, ho! My lord! My lady!

Enter LADY CAPULET

LADY CAPULET What noise is here?
NURSE O lamentable day!
LADY CAPULET What is the matter?
NURSE Look, look! O heavy day!
LADY CAPULET O me, O me! My child, my only life,
Revive, look up, or I will die with thee!
Help, help! Call help.

Enter CAPULET

CAPULET For shame, bring Juliet forth — her lord is come.
NURSE She's dead, deceased, she's dead — alack the day!
LADY CAPULET Alack the day, she's dead, she's dead, she's dead!
CAPULET Ha! Let me see her. Out, alas! She's cold.
Her blood is settled, and her joints are stiff,
Life and these lips have long been separated:
Death lies on her like an untimely frost
Upon the sweetest flower of all the field.
NURSE O lamentable day!

nurse's own mini tragedy
nurse may feel guilt for betraying Juliet
↳ she can't say sorry
audience pity her - although she betrayed her.

2 'slug-a-bed' means 'lazybones'.

4 'pennyworths' means 'small amounts'.

Shakespeare's Techniques

The Nurse makes crude comments about Juliet not getting any sleep on her wedding night. The Nurse's humour adds to the dramatic tension of the scene.

17 'lamentable' means 'miserable'.

Shakespeare's Techniques

The repetition of 'dead' changes the mood of the scene to shock and sorrow.

Act 4, Scene 5

31 'ta'en' means 'taken'.

Shakespeare's Techniques

Capulet echoes the image of death as Juliet's bridegroom. This foreshadows the death of his real son-in-law, Romeo.

Character — Capulet

Capulet doesn't have any other children to inherit his wealth and status — Capulet's legacy has died with Juliet.

46-48 'My only child was my only happiness, and now death has taken her away from me.'

Character — Lady Capulet

Lady Capulet sounds genuinely distressed. This contrasts with the way she rejected Juliet earlier, in Act 3, Scene 5 (lines 140 and 203).

60-61 'Why now, to ruin our celebration?'

64 'My happiness is buried with my child.'

65-66 'This disaster won't be solved by this chaos.'

69 By 'Your part' he means 'Juliet's body'.

70 By 'his part' he means 'Juliet's soul'.

71 'promotion' here means 'advancement in society'.

LADY CAPULET O woeful time!

CAPULET Death, that hath ta'en her hence to make me wail,
Ties up my tongue, and will not let me speak.

Enter FRIAR LAWRENCE *and* PARIS, *with Musicians*

FRIAR LAWRENCE Come, is the bride ready to go to church?

CAPULET Ready to go, but never to return.
O son! The night before thy wedding day
Hath Death lain with thy wife. There she lies,
Flower as she was, deflowerèd by him.
Death is my son-in-law, Death is my heir;
My daughter he hath wedded. I will die,
And leave him all; life, living, all is Death's.

PARIS Have I thought long to see this morning's face,
And doth it give me such a sight as this?

LADY CAPULET Accursed, unhappy, wretched, hateful day!
Most miserable hour that e'er time saw
In lasting labour of his pilgrimage!
But one, poor one, one poor and loving child,
But one thing to rejoice and solace in,
And cruel death hath catched it from my sight!

NURSE O woe! O woeful, woeful, woeful day!
Most lamentable day, most woeful day,
That ever, ever, I did yet behold!
O day! O day! O day! O hateful day!
Never was seen so black a day as this.
O woeful day, O woeful day!

PARIS Beguiled, divorcèd, wrongèd, spited, slain!
Most detestable death, by thee beguiled,
By cruel, cruel, thee, quite overthrown!
O love! O life! Not life, but love in death!

CAPULET Despised, distressèd, hated, martyred, killed!
Uncomfortable time, why camest thou now
To murder, murder our solemnity?
O child! O child! My soul, and not my child!
Dead art thou! Alack! My child is dead,
And with my child my joys are buried.

FRIAR LAWRENCE Peace, ho, for shame. Confusion's cure lives not
In these confusions. Heaven and yourself
Had part in this fair maid — now heaven hath all,
And all the better is it for the maid:
Your part in her you could not keep from death,
But heaven keeps his part in eternal life.
The most you sought was her promotion;
For 'twas your heaven she should be advanced:
And weep ye now, seeing she is advanced
Above the clouds, as high as heaven itself?
O, in this love, you love your child so ill,
That you run mad, seeing that she is well:

Act 4, Scene 5

She's not well married that lives married long,
But she's best married that dies married young.
Dry up your tears, and stick your rosemary
On this fair corse; and, as the custom is,
In all her best array bear her to church:
For though fond nature bids us all lament,
Yet nature's tears are reason's merriment.

CAPULET All things that we ordainèd festival,
Turn from their office to black funeral,
Our instruments to melancholy bells,
Our wedding cheer to a sad burial feast,
Our solemn hymns to sullen dirges change,
Our bridal flowers serve for a buried corse,
And all things change them to the contrary.

FRIAR LAWRENCE Sir, go you in, and, madam, go with him,
And go, Sir Paris. Everyone prepare
To follow this fair corse unto her grave:
The heavens do lower upon you for some ill;
Move them no more by crossing their high will.

Exeunt CAPULET, LADY CAPULET, PARIS, *and* FRIAR LAWRENCE

FIRST MUSICIAN Faith, we may put up our pipes, and be gone.

NURSE Honest goodfellows, ah, put up, put up,
For, well you know, this is a pitiful case.

Exit

FIRST MUSICIAN Ay, by my troth, the case may be amended.

Enter PETER

PETER Musicians, O, musicians, 'Heart's ease', Heart's ease': O, and you will have me live, play 'Heart's ease'.

FIRST MUSICIAN Why 'Heart's ease'?

PETER O, musicians, because my heart itself plays 'My heart is full of woe'. O, play me some merry dump, to comfort me.

FIRST MUSICIAN Not a dump we; 'tis no time to play now.

PETER You will not, then?

FIRST MUSICIAN No.

PETER I will then give it you soundly.

FIRST MUSICIAN What will you give us?

PETER No money, on my faith, but the gleek. I will give you the minstrel.

FIRST MUSICIAN Then will I give you the serving-creature.

PETER Then will I lay the serving-creature's dagger on your pate. I will carry no crotchets, I'll re you, I'll fa you, do you note me?

FIRST MUSICIAN And you re us and fa us, you note us.

SECOND MUSICIAN Pray you, put up your dagger, and put out your wit.

PETER Then have at you with my wit! I will dry-beat you with an iron wit, and put up my iron dagger. Answer me like men:
'When griping grief the heart doth wound,

Character — Friar Lawrence

The Friar encourages the Capulets to take Juliet's body to the tomb. He's trying to move his plan along.

84-85 All the things we ordered for the wedding need to be made appropriate for the funeral'.

Shakespeare's Techniques

Capulet repeats "all things" and "our" and uses alliteration in the words "solemn" / "sullen" and "bridal" / "burial". Capulet's poetic language emphasises his sadness and demonstrates the dignified side to his character.

98-99 The Nurse comments that Juliet's death is a sad case. The musician misinterprets what she means — he thinks that the Nurse is remarking that his instrument case is shabby.

100-101 Peter wants to hear a song called 'Heart's Ease'.

104 'merry dump' means 'a sad song which is happy' — he's contradicting himself.

110 'gleek' means 'rude sign'.

Shakespeare's Techniques

The comical dialogue, in prose, adds some humour to this solemn scene. This gives the audience a bit of light relief before the tragedy of Act 5.

114 're' and 'fa' are musical notes.

Act 4, Scene 5

And doleful dumps the mind oppress,
Then music with her silver sound' —
Why 'silver sound'? Why 'music with her silver sound'?
What say you, Simon Catling?

FIRST MUSICIAN Marry, sir, because silver hath a sweet sound.

PETER Pretty! What say you, Hugh Rebeck?

SECOND MUSICIAN I say 'silver sound', because musicians sound for silver.

PETER Pretty too! What say you, James Soundpost?

THIRD MUSICIAN Faith, I know not what to say.

PETER O, I cry you mercy, you are the singer. I will say for you. It is 'music with her silver sound', because musicians have no gold for sounding:
'Then music with her silver sound
With speedy help doth lend redress.'

Exit

FIRST MUSICIAN What a pestilent knave is this same!

SECOND MUSICIAN Hang him, Jack! Come, we'll in here, tarry for the mourners, and stay dinner.

Exeunt

124 'Catling' means 'catgut', which was used for making the strings of musical instruments.

126 'Rebeck' is a type of fiddle.

129 'Soundpost' is a part of a fiddle.

136 'What an annoying idiot he was'.

137-138 'Forget him Jack. Come on, we'll go in here, wait for the mourners and then stay for dinner'.

Performance

The comic dialogue between Peter and the musicians seems out of place in what is quite a sad scene. The original stage direction after line 99 was "*Enter Will Kemp*". Kemp was a famous comic performer in Shakespeare's day, so it's possible that this exchange was added to the scene to give Kemp a chance to entertain the audience.

Act Four — Practice Questions

Quick Questions

1) Which two characters visit Friar Lawrence in Act 4, Scene 1?

2) Who gives Juliet the potion?

3) How does Friar Lawrence intend to tell Romeo about the plan?

4) Why does Juliet think that her potion might be poisonous?

5) The wedding is brought forward by:
 a) a week b) a day c) 4 hours

6) Who discovers Juliet's 'dead' body?

7) What is the name of the song that Peter wants to hear?

8) Find two props mentioned in the stage directions of Act 4.

In-depth Questions

1) Describe how Juliet's mood changes during Act 4, Scene 1.

2) Do you think Juliet is acting desperately or bravely when she agrees to the Friar's plan? Explain your answer.

3) How does Shakespeare use language to emphasise the characters' grief in Act 4, Scene 5?

4) How does the mood change between Scene 4 and Scene 5? Why do you think Shakespeare chose to put these two scenes next to each other?

5) Do you think Friar Lawrence's plan to fake Juliet's death is cruel or necessary? Explain your answer.

6) In Act 4, Scene 3 Juliet is scared that the potion might kill her. Imagine you are Juliet — write a letter to Romeo just before you drink the potion, telling him your last wishes and your dying thoughts and feelings.

7) Imagine you are a film director. You want to show Juliet's terror in Act 4, Scene 3 as much as possible. Write some instructions for the cast and crew, describing how you want the scene to look and be acted.

Act 5, Scene 1 — Romeo Thinks Juliet's Dead

Romeo is in Mantua, waiting for news of Juliet. His servant, Balthasar, tells him that Juliet is dead. Romeo and Balthasar don't know about the Friar's plan. Romeo decides to buy some poison and kill himself in Juliet's tomb.

ACT 5, SCENE 1

MANTUA. A STREET.

Enter ROMEO

ROMEO If I may trust the flattering truth of sleep,
My dreams presage some joyful news at hand.
My bosom's lord sits lightly in his throne,
And all this day an unaccustomed spirit
Lifts me above the ground with cheerful thoughts.
I dreamt my lady came and found me dead —
Strange dream, that gives a dead man leave to think! —
And breathed such life with kisses in my lips,
That I revived, and was an emperor.
Ah me! How sweet is love itself possessed,
When but love's shadows are so rich in joy!

Enter BALTHASAR, *booted*

News from Verona! How now, Balthasar!
Dost thou not bring me letters from the Friar?
How doth my lady? Is my father well?
How fares my Juliet? That I ask again,
For nothing can be ill, if she be well.

BALTHASAR Then she is well, and nothing can be ill.
Her body sleeps in Capel's monument,
And her immortal part with angels lives.
I saw her laid low in her kindred's vault,
And presently took post to tell it you.
O, pardon me for bringing these ill news,
Since you did leave it for my office, sir.

ROMEO Is it e'en so? Then I defy you, stars!
Thou know'st my lodging: get me ink and paper,
And hire post-horses. I will hence tonight.

BALTHASAR I do beseech you, sir, have patience.
Your looks are pale and wild, and do import
Some misadventure.

ROMEO Tush, thou art deceived.
Leave me, and do the thing I bid thee do.
Hast thou no letters to me from the Friar?

BALTHASAR No, my good lord.

ROMEO No matter. Get thee gone,

2 'presage' means 'foretell'.

3 'My heart is light in my chest.' (I'm in good spirits.)

Shakespeare's Techniques

Romeo had a dream that he was dead, but that Juliet's kiss brought him back to life. This foreshadows Romeo's death at the end of the play.

16 'Nothing can be wrong, if she is okay.'

23 'give me this duty'.

Theme — Fate

Romeo thinks fate is against him. However, it's his decision to return to Verona that leads to his and Juliet's deaths.

28-29 'You look mad, as if you're going to do something reckless.'

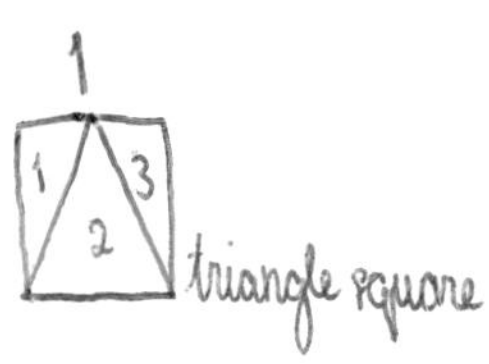

Act 5, Scene 1

And hire those horses. I'll be with thee straight.

Exit BALTHASAR

Well, Juliet, I will lie with thee tonight.
Let's see for means. O mischief, thou art swift
To enter in the thoughts of desperate men!
I do remember an apothecary —
And hereabouts he dwells — which late I noted
In tattered weeds, with overwhelming brows,
Culling of simples. Meagre were his looks,
Sharp misery had worn him to the bones,
And in his needy shop a tortoise hung,
An alligator stuffed, and other skins
Of ill-shaped fishes; and about his shelves
A beggarly account of empty boxes,
Green earthen pots, bladders and musty seeds,
Remnants of packthread and old cakes of roses,
Were thinly scattered, to make up a show.
Noting this penury, to myself I said
'And if a man did need a poison now,
Whose sale is present death in Mantua,
Here lives a caitiff wretch would sell it him.'
O, this same thought did but forerun my need,
And this same needy man must sell it me.
As I remember, this should be the house.
Being holiday, the beggar's shop is shut.
What, ho! Apothecary!

Enter APOTHECARY

APOTHECARY Who calls so loud?

ROMEO Come hither, man. I see that thou art poor.
Hold, there is forty ducats. Let me have
A dram of poison, such soon-speeding gear
As will disperse itself through all the veins
That the life-weary taker may fall dead
And that the trunk may be discharged of breath
As violently as hasty powder fired
Doth hurry from the fatal cannon's womb.

APOTHECARY Such mortal drugs I have, but Mantua's law
Is death to any he that utters them.

ROMEO Art thou so bare and full of wretchedness,
And fear'st to die? Famine is in thy cheeks,
Need and oppression starveth in thine eyes,
Contempt and beggary hangs upon thy back.
The world is not thy friend nor the world's law,
The world affords no law to make thee rich;
Then be not poor, but break it, and take this.

APOTHECARY My poverty, but not my will, consents.

ROMEO I pay thy poverty, and not thy will.

APOTHECARY Put this in any liquid thing you will,
And drink it off; and, if you had the strength

35 'Let's work out how.'

35 'mischief' means 'wickedness'.

37 An 'apothecary' was someone who made and sold medicines and drugs.

39 'weeds' means 'clothes'.

40 'Collecting herbs (for medicine).'

47 'packthread' is string used for tying packages.

49 'penury' means 'poverty'.

52 'caitiff' means 'miserable'.

Shakespeare's Techniques

This echoes Lady Capulet's hope that Romeo would be poisoned by "an unaccustomed dram" as revenge for Tybalt's death (Act 3, Scene 5, line 90).

60 'fast-acting poison'

67 'utters' means 'sells'.

Character — Romeo

Romeo's determination to commit suicide is made clear by the way he takes advantage of the apothecary's poverty to get the poison.

Act 5, Scene 2 — The Friar's Message Fails

Of twenty men, it would dispatch you straight.

ROMEO There is thy gold, worse poison to men's souls,
Doing more murders in this loathsome world,
Than these poor compounds that thou mayst not sell.
I sell thee poison, thou hast sold me none.
Farewell, buy food, and get thyself in flesh.

Exit APOTHECARY

Come, cordial and not poison, go with me
To Juliet's grave; for there must I use thee.

Exit

85 'cordial' was a medicine that stimulated the heart.

Shakespeare's Techniques

Putting these two short scenes in between long ones makes it seem like things are happening very quickly. This makes it feel like everything is getting out of control.

The Friar finds out that his letter to Romeo never arrived — he doesn't know that Romeo thinks that Juliet's dead. He decides to go to the tomb to be there when Juliet wakes up.

ACT 5, SCENE 2

short scene to speed things up - accelerating to death

FRIAR LAWRENCE'S CELL

Enter FRIAR JOHN

FRIAR JOHN Holy Franciscan Friar! Brother, ho!

Enter FRIAR LAWRENCE

FRIAR LAWRENCE This same should be the voice of Friar John.
Welcome from Mantua. What says Romeo?
Or, if his mind be writ, give me his letter.

FRIAR JOHN Going to find a barefoot brother out
One of our order, to associate me,
Here in this city visiting the sick,
And finding him, the searchers of the town,
Suspecting that we both were in a house
Where the Infectious pestilence did reign,
Sealed up the doors, and would not let us forth,
So that my speed to Mantua there was stayed.

FRIAR LAWRENCE Who bare my letter, then, to Romeo?

FRIAR JOHN I could not send it — here it is again —
Nor get a messenger to bring it thee,
So fearful were they of infection.

FRIAR LAWRENCE Unhappy fortune! By my brotherhood,
The letter was not nice but full of charge
Of dear import, and the neglecting it
May do much danger. Friar John, go hence,
Get me an iron crow, and bring it straight
Unto my cell. → needs to open the tomb

FRIAR JOHN Brother, I'll go and bring it thee.

Exit

4 'Or, if his message is written down, give me his letter.'

5-12 Friar John explains that when he went to find another friar to go with him, the health officers held them, in case they were carrying an infectious disease. He hasn't been able to leave the city

Theme — Fate

Friar Lawrence couldn't control this event, which suggests that the lovers are doomed to be unlucky.

18-19 'full of things that are very important...'

21 'crow' means 'crowbar'.

Act 5, Scene 3 — The Final Scene

FRIAR LAWRENCE Now must I to the monument alone,
Within this three hours will fair Juliet wake.
She will beshrew me much that Romeo
Hath had no notice of these accidents,
But I will write again to Mantua,
And keep her at my cell till Romeo come.
Poor living corse, closed in a dead man's tomb!

Exit

technique - running out of time

24 'monument' means 'tomb'.

Shakespeare's Techniques

Although the prologue has told us how the play ends, Shakespeare keeps hope alive — Friar Lawrence might meet Romeo at the tomb, or Juliet might wake up in time.

26-27 'She will curse me for not warning Romeo about these events.'

Paris sees Romeo going into Juliet's tomb, and they fight. Romeo kills Paris and drinks the poison. The Friar arrives just as Juliet wakes up, and they see that Romeo is dead. After Friar Lawrence leaves, Juliet kills herself. The Montagues and the Capulets arrive at the tomb and discover that their children are dead. The Friar explains what has happened, and the two families realise that their feud has caused the two deaths. They make peace.

ACT 5, SCENE 3

Shakespeare kills Paris so we can focus on Romeo and Juliet.

A CHURCHYARD — IN IT A TOMB
BELONGING TO THE CAPULETS

Enter PARIS, *and his* PAGE *bearing flowers and a torch*

PARIS Give me thy torch, boy. Hence, and stand aloof.
Yet put it out, for I would not be seen.
Under yond yew trees lay thee all along,
Holding thine ear close to the hollow ground,
So shall no foot upon the churchyard tread,
Being loose, unfirm, with digging up of graves,
But thou shalt hear it. Whistle then to me,
As signal that thou hear'st something approach.
Give me those flowers. Do as I bid thee, go.

PAGE (*Aside*) I am almost afraid to stand alone
Here in the churchyard, yet I will adventure.

Retires

PARIS Sweet flower, with flowers thy bridal bed I strew —
O woe! Thy canopy is dust and stones —
Which with sweet water nightly I will dew,
Or, wanting that, with tears distilled by moans.
The obsequies that I for thee will keep
Nightly shall be to strew thy grave and weep.

The PAGE *whistles*

The boy gives warning something doth approach.
What cursèd foot wanders this way tonight,
To cross my obsequies and true love's rite?
What with a torch! Muffle me, night, awhile.

Retires

Enter ROMEO *and* BALTHASAR,
with a torch, mattock and a crow of iron

ROMEO Give me that mattock and the wrenching iron.

4-7 'Put your ear close to the ground so that you can hear if anyone comes into the churchyard.'

Shakespeare's Technique

Paris's grief makes this moment sad, but also quite calm. This contrasts with the panic that comes before, and the chaos that comes after.

14-15 'I'll sprinkle perfumed water every night on your grave, or, if I don't have that, I'll use tears.'

16 'obsequies' means 'funeral rites'.

bad poetry like Romeo's love for Rosaline → cliché - makes himself believe he loves her. → deliberate contrast to Romeo

22 a 'mattock' is a tool like a pickaxe.

Act 5, Scene 3

Hold, take this letter — early in the morning
See thou deliver it to my lord and father.
Give me the light: upon thy life, I charge thee,
Whate'er thou hear'st or seest, stand all aloof,
And do not interrupt me in my course.
Why I descend into this bed of death,
Is partly to behold my lady's face,
But chiefly to take thence from her dead finger
A precious ring, a ring that I must use
In dear employment: therefore hence, be gone.
But if thou, jealous, dost return to pry
In what I farther shall intend to do,
By heaven, I will tear thee joint by joint
And strew this hungry churchyard with thy limbs.
The time and my intents are savage-wild,
More fierce and more inexorable far
Than empty tigers or the roaring sea.

BALTHASAR I will be gone, sir, and not trouble you.

ROMEO So shalt thou show me friendship. Take thou that:
Live, and be prosperous, and farewell, good fellow.

BALTHASAR (*Aside*) For all this same, I'll hide me hereabout:
His looks I fear, and his intents I doubt.

Retires

ROMEO Thou detestable maw, thou womb of death,
Gorged with the dearest morsel of the earth,
Thus I enforce thy rotten jaws to open,
And, in despite, I'll cram thee with more food!

Opens the tomb

PARIS This is that banished haughty Montague,
That murdered my love's cousin, with which grief,
It is supposèd, the fair creature died,
And here is come to do some villainous shame
To the dead bodies. I will apprehend him.

Comes forward

Stop thy unhallowed toil, vile Montague!
Can vengeance be pursued further than death?
Condemnèd villain, I do apprehend thee.
Obey, and go with me; for thou must die.

ROMEO I must indeed, and therefore came I hither.
Good gentle youth, tempt not a desperate man.
Fly hence, and leave me: think upon these gone.
Let them affright thee. I beseech thee, youth,
Put not another sin upon my head,
By urging me to fury. O, be gone!
By heaven, I love thee better than myself,
For I come hither armed against myself.
Stay not, be gone; live, and hereafter say,
A madman's mercy bid thee run away.

PARIS I do defy thy conjuration,

30-32 Romeo lies to Balthasar about why he's going to see Juliet. It's possible he does this to stop Balthasar from following him.

37 'intents' means 'plans'.

38 'inexorable' means 'unstoppable'.

Theme — Love

This scene contrasts Romeo and Paris's reactions to Juliet's death. Paris's grief is conventional — he's solemn and respectful, whereas Romeo is desperate and aggressive.

45 'maw' means 'mouth'.

49 'haughty' means 'arrogant'.

50-51 Paris believes Romeo is the cause of Juliet's death — he thinks she died of sadness over Tybalt's death.

53 'apprehend' means 'arrest'.

54 'unhallowed toil' means 'unholy work'.

59-63 Romeo pleads with Paris not to make him fight, because he doesn't want to kill him.

68 'defy thy conjuration' means 'refuse your appeal'.

Act 5, Scene 3

And apprehend thee for a felon here.
ROMEO Wilt thou provoke me? Then have at thee, boy!

They fight

PAGE O Lord, they fight! I will go call the watch.

Exit

PARIS O, I am slain!

Falls

If thou be merciful,
Open the tomb, lay me with Juliet.

Dies

ROMEO In faith, I will. Let me peruse this face.
Mercutio's kinsman, noble County Paris!
What said my man, when my betossèd soul
Did not attend him as we rode? I think
He told me Paris should have married Juliet.
Said he not so? Or did I dream it so?
Or am I mad, hearing him talk of Juliet,
To think it was so? O, give me thy hand,
One writ with me in sour misfortune's book!
I'll bury thee in a triumphant grave.
A grave? O no! A lantern, slaughtered youth,
For here lies Juliet, and her beauty makes
This vault a feasting presence full of light.
Death, lie thou there, by a dead man interred.

Laying PARIS *in the tomb*

How oft when men are at the point of death
Have they been merry! Which their keepers call
A lightning before death: O, how may I
Call this a lightning? O my love! My wife!
Death, that hath sucked the honey of thy breath,
Hath had no power yet upon thy beauty.
Thou art not conquered. Beauty's ensign yet
Is crimson in thy lips and in thy cheeks,
And death's pale flag is not advancèd there.
Tybalt, liest thou there in thy bloody sheet?
O, what more favour can I do to thee,
Than with that hand that cut thy youth in twain
To sunder his that was thine enemy?
Forgive me, cousin! Ah, dear Juliet,
Why art thou yet so fair? Shall I believe
That unsubstantial death is amorous,
And that the lean abhorrèd monster keeps
Thee here in dark to be his paramour?
For fear of that, I still will stay with thee,
And never from this palace of dim night
Depart again. Here, here will I remain
With worms that are thy chambermaids. O, here
Will I set up my everlasting rest,
And shake the yoke of inauspicious stars

69 'felon' means 'criminal'.

Theme — Conflict

Paris's death adds to the tragedy of the play — he is another young victim.

74 'peruse' means 'look at'.

76 'betossèd' means 'disturbed'.

77 'Did not listen to him...'

81-82 'Give me your hand, you're as unlucky as I am.'

Shakespeare's Techniques

Romeo uses images of light to describe Juliet throughout the play (such as Act 1, Scene 5, line 43). This emphasises how, for Romeo, Juliet's beauty stands out from everything else.

88-89 'Men often feel happy when they're about to die.'

Shakespeare's Techniques

Romeo wonders how Juliet can still be so beautiful — she looks as if she's not dead. This is dramatic irony — the audience knows she's alive, and it's very tense because she could wake up at any moment.

104 'abhorrèd' means 'hated'. Romeo is talking about Death.

105 'paramour' means 'lover'.

109-111 'I'll stay here forever and shake off my bad luck.'

Act 5, Scene 3

114-118 'This kiss will seal my eternal deal with death. Come on poison, guide me to death. You desperate sailor, let's crash this world-weary boat into the rocks.'

Theme — Love

The final line of Romeo's soliloquy echoes the words of Juliet in Act 4, Scene 3 (line 58) as she drinks the potion — "Here's drink — I drink to thee."

From this world-wearied flesh. Eyes, look your last!
Arms, take your last embrace! And, lips, O you
The doors of breath, seal with a righteous kiss
A dateless bargain to engrossing death!
Come, bitter conduct, come, unsavoury guide!
Thou desperate pilot, now at once run on
The dashing rocks thy seasick weary bark!
Here's to my love!

Drinks

O true apothecary!
Thy drugs are quick. Thus with a kiss I die.

Dies

Enter, at the other end of the churchyard, FRIAR LAWRENCE, *with a lantern, crow, and spade*

FRIAR LAWRENCE Saint Francis be my speed! How oft tonight
Have my old feet stumbled at graves! Who's there?

BALTHASAR Here's one, a friend, and one that knows you well.

Shakespeare's Techniques

Friar Lawrence's horrible language sets the mood for the rest of scene.

FRIAR LAWRENCE Bliss be upon you! Tell me, good my friend,
What torch is yond, that vainly lends his light
To grubs and eyeless skulls? As I discern,
It burneth in the Capel's monument.

127 the 'Capel's monument' is the 'Capulet's tomb'.

BALTHASAR It doth so, holy sir, and there's my master,
One that you love.

FRIAR LAWRENCE Who is it?

BALTHASAR Romeo.

FRIAR LAWRENCE How long hath he been there?

BALTHASAR Full half an hour.

FRIAR LAWRENCE Go with me to the vault.

BALTHASAR I dare not, sir
My master knows not but I am gone hence,
And fearfully did menace me with death,
If I did stay to look on his intents.

132-134 'My master thinks I've gone, and he threatened to kill me if I stayed to see what he was up to.'

FRIAR LAWRENCE Stay, then; I'll go alone. Fear comes upon me.
O, much I fear some ill unthrifty thing.

136 'unthrifty' means 'unlucky'.

BALTHASAR As I did sleep under this yew tree here,
I dreamt my master and another fought,
And that my master slew him.

FRIAR LAWRENCE Romeo!

Advances

Alack, alack, what blood is this, which stains
The stony entrance of this sepulchre?
What mean these masterless and gory swords
To lie discoloured by this place of peace?

141 'sepulchre' means 'tomb'.

142-143 'Why are there abandoned and bloody swords near this peaceful place?'

Enters the tomb

Romeo! O, pale! Who else? What, Paris too?
And steeped in blood? Ah, what an unkind hour
Is guilty of this lamentable chance!

146 'lamentable' means 'sad'.

Act 5, Scene 3

The lady stirs.

JULIET wakes

JULIET O comfortable Friar! Where is my lord?
I do remember well where I should be,
And there I am. Where is my Romeo?

Noise within

FRIAR LAWRENCE I hear some noise. Lady, come from that nest
Of death, contagion, and unnatural sleep.
A greater power than we can contradict
Hath thwarted our intents. Come, come away.
Thy husband in thy bosom there lies dead,
And Paris too. Come, I'll dispose of thee
Among a sisterhood of holy nuns.
Stay not to question, for the watch is coming;
Come, go, good Juliet,

Noise again

I dare no longer stay.

JULIET Go, get thee hence, for I will not away.

Exit FRIAR LAWRENCE

What's here? A cup, closed in my true love's hand?
Poison, I see, hath been his timeless end.
O churl! Drunk all, and left no friendly drop
To help me after? I will kiss thy lips,
Haply some poison yet doth hang on them,
To make me die with a restorative.

Kisses him

Thy lips are warm.

FIRST WATCHMAN (*Within*) Lead, boy, which way?

JULIET Yea, noise? Then I'll be brief. O happy dagger!

Snatching ROMEO's dagger

This is thy sheath.

Stabs herself

There rust, and let me die.

Falls on ROMEO's body, and dies

Enter WATCHMEN, with the PAGE of Paris

PAGE This is the place, there where the torch doth burn.

FIRST WATCHMAN The ground is bloody, search about the churchyard:
Go, some of you, whoe'er you find attach.

Exeunt some of the WATCHMEN

Pitiful sight! Here lies the county slain,
And Juliet bleeding, warm, and newly dead,
Who here hath lain these two days burièd.
Go, tell the Prince, run to the Capulets:
Raise up the Montagues. Some others search.

Exeunt other WATCHMEN

148 'comfortable' means 'comforting'.

Theme — Fate

By 'greater power' the Friar could mean God. He's suggesting that the tragedy was unavoidable — the forces working against them were too powerful.

156-157 The Friar wants to take Juliet to a convent.

160 'You go — I am not leaving'.

163 'churl' means 'rude man'.

Shakespeare's Techniques

Juliet kisses Romeo's lips, hoping that she can share some of the poison — this reminds the audience of Romeo's dream in Act 5, Scene 1 (lines 6-9).

169 'happy' means 'fortunate'.

Character — Juliet

Juliet gave a speech about death before she took the potion, but she doesn't have one here. This makes her actions seem panicked — she wants to kill herself before someone arrives and tries to stop her.

173 'arrest whoever you find.'

Act 5, Scene 3

179-181 'We see the ground the bodies lie on, but it's hard to say what the real cause of their deaths was.'

We see the ground whereon these woes do lie,
But the true ground of all these piteous woes
We cannot without circumstance descry.

Re-enter some of the WATCHMEN, *with* BALTHASAR

SECOND WATCHMAN Here's Romeo's man, we found him in the churchyard.

183 'Keep him in custody until the Prince arrives'.

FIRST WATCHMAN Hold him in safety, till the Prince come hither.

Re-enter other WATCHMEN, *with* FRIAR LAWRENCE

THIRD WATCHMAN Here is a friar, that trembles, sighs and weeps:
We took this mattock and this spade from him,
As he was coming from this churchyard side.

187 'stay' means 'hold'.

FIRST WATCHMAN A great suspicion. Stay the friar too.

Enter the PRINCE *and Attendants*

188-189 'What's going on, to get me out of bed so early?'

PRINCE What misadventure is so early up,
That calls our person from our morning rest?

Enter CAPULET, LADY CAPULET *and others*

190 'What's everyone shouting about?'

CAPULET What should it be, that they so shriek abroad?

LADY CAPULET The people in the street cry 'Romeo',
Some 'Juliet', and some 'Paris', and all run,
With open outcry toward our monument.

PRINCE What fear is this which startles in our ears?

FIRST WATCHMAN Sovereign, here lies the County Paris slain,
And Romeo dead, and Juliet, dead before,
Warm and new killed.

PRINCE Search, seek, and know how this foul murder comes.

FIRST WATCHMAN Here is a friar, and slaughtered Romeo's man,
With instruments upon them, fit to open
These dead men's tombs.

203-205 'This dagger's gone the wrong way. It should be in the sheath on Romeo's back, but it's stabbed in Juliet's chest.'

CAPULET O heavens! O wife, look how our daughter bleeds!
This dagger hath mista'en, for, lo, his house
Is empty on the back of Montague,
And it mis-sheathèd in my daughter's bosom!

LADY CAPULET O me! This sight of death is as a bell,
That warns my old age to a sepulchre.

Shakespeare's Technique

This part of the scene is quite chaotic with most of the characters on stage. They all learn about the deaths at different points, emphasising just how many people are affected by what's happened.

Enter MONTAGUE *and others*

PRINCE Come, Montague; for thou art early up,
To see thy son and heir more early down.

MONTAGUE Alas, my liege, my wife is dead tonight.
Grief of my son's exile hath stopped her breath.
What further woe conspires against mine age?

PRINCE Look, and thou shalt see.

214-215 Montague is upset that Romeo has died before him.

MONTAGUE O thou untaught! What manners is in this?
To press before thy father to a grave?

217 'ambiguities' means 'uncertainties' or 'questions'.

PRINCE Seal up the mouth of outrage for a while,
Till we can clear these ambiguities,
And know their spring, their head, their true descent,
And then will I be general of your woes,

Act 5, Scene 3

And lead you even to death. Meantime forbear,
And let mischance be slave to patience.
Bring forth the parties of suspicion.

FRIAR LAWRENCE I am the greatest, able to do least,
Yet most suspected, as the time and place
Doth make against me of this direful murder.
And here I stand, both to impeach and purge
Myself condemnèd and myself excused.

PRINCE Then say at once what thou dost know in this.

FRIAR LAWRENCE I will be brief, for my short date of breath
Is not so long as is a tedious tale.
Romeo, there dead, was husband to that Juliet,
And she, there dead, that Romeo's faithful wife.
I married them, and their stol'n marriage day
Was Tybalt's doomsday, whose untimely death
Banished the new-made bridegroom from the city,
For whom, and not for Tybalt, Juliet pined.
You, to remove that siege of grief from her,
Betrothed and would have married her perforce
To County Paris: then comes she to me,
And, with wild looks, bid me devise some mean
To rid her from this second marriage,
Or in my cell there would she kill herself.
Then gave I her, so tutored by my art,
A sleeping potion, which so took effect
As I intended, for it wrought on her
The form of death. Meantime I writ to Romeo,
That he should hither come as this dire night,
To help to take her from her borrowed grave,
Being the time the potion's force should cease.
But he which bore my letter, Friar John,
Was stayed by accident, and yesternight
Returned my letter back. Then all alone
At the prefixèd hour of her waking,
Came I to take her from her kindred's vault,
Meaning to keep her closely at my cell,
Till I conveniently could send to Romeo:
But when I came, some minute ere the time
Of her awaking, here untimely lay
The noble Paris and true Romeo dead.
She wakes; and I entreated her come forth,
And bear this work of heaven with patience,
But then a noise did scare me from the tomb,
And she, too desperate, would not go with me,
But, as it seems, did violence on herself.
All this I know, and to the marriage
Her nurse is privy, and, if aught in this
Miscarried by my fault, let my old life
Be sacrificed, some hour before his time,
Unto the rigour of severest law.

PRINCE We still have known thee for a holy man.

221 'accept your misfortune with patience.'

223-227 'I'm the biggest suspect if you look at the evidence, and I am the most powerless. I stand here to both accuse myself and clear my name.'

229-230 Something like, 'my life isn't going to be long enough to tell a boring story.'

233 'stol'n' means 'secret'.

237 'siege' means 'onslaught' or 'attack'.

238 'perforce' means 'by force'.

243 'art' means 'skills'.

251 'yesternight' means 'last night'.

253 'prefixèd' means 'prearranged'.

254 'kindred's' means 'family's'.

Shakespeare's Techniques

The Friar recaps what has happened. His speech slows down the pace of the play as it draws to an end.

266 'is privy' means 'knows about it'.

Act 5, Scene 3

Where's Romeo's man? What can he say in this?
BALTHASAR I brought my master news of Juliet's death,
And then in post he came from Mantua
To this same place, to this same monument.
This letter he early bid me give his father,
And threatened me with death, going in the vault,
If I departed not and left him there.
PRINCE Give me the letter, I will look on it.
Where is the County's page, that raised the watch?
Sirrah, what made your master in this place?
PAGE He came with flowers to strew his lady's grave,
And bid me stand aloof, and so I did.
Anon comes one with light to ope the tomb,
And by and by my master drew on him,
And then I ran away to call the watch.
PRINCE This letter doth make good the Friar's words,
Their course of love, the tidings of her death,
And here he writes that he did buy a poison
Of a poor 'pothecary, and therewithal
Came to this vault to die, and lie with Juliet.
Where be these enemies? Capulet! Montague!
See, what a scourge is laid upon your hate,
That heaven finds means to kill your joys with love.
And I for winking at your discords too
Have lost a brace of kinsmen. All are punished.
CAPULET O brother Montague, give me thy hand:
This is my daughter's jointure, for no more
Can I demand.
MONTAGUE But I can give thee more,
For I will raise her statue in pure gold,
That whiles Verona by that name is known,
There shall no figure at such rate be set
As that of true and faithful Juliet.
CAPULET As rich shall Romeo's by his lady's lie,
Poor sacrifices of our enmity!
PRINCE A glooming peace this morning with it brings,
The sun, for sorrow, will not show his head.
Go hence, to have more talk of these sad things.
Some shall be pardoned, and some punished,
For never was a story of more woe
Than this of Juliet and her Romeo.
Exeunt

273 'in post' means 'quickly'.

275 'early' means 'as soon as possible'.

280 'why was your master here?'

286 'This letter backs up the Friar's statement.'

292 'scourge' means 'punishment'.

Theme — Fate

The Prince blames the family feud for their loss — 'heaven' (or fate) has found a way to punish the families.

294-295 'And I, by shutting my eyes to your feud, have lost two relatives (Mercutio and Paris).'

Theme — Conflict

Although the play has a tragic ending, the conflict between the two families has ended.

297 A 'jointure' is a payment (or property) paid to a bride to support her if her husband dies.

Act Five — Practice Questions

Quick Questions

1) Who tells Romeo that Juliet is dead in Act 5, Scene 1?
2) Why doesn't Romeo know about the Friar's plan?
3) What does Paris think that Romeo is doing at the tomb?
4) What is Paris's dying wish?
5) How does Romeo die?
6) Who is with Juliet in the tomb when she wakes up?
7) How does Juliet die?
8) Who has died of grief because of Romeo's banishment?
9) What does Montague promise to build in memory of Juliet?

In-depth Questions

1) Friar Lawrence gives Juliet a chance to escape the tomb but she decides to kill herself instead. Give three reasons why you think she makes this decision.
2) Who do you think is to blame for Romeo and Juliet's deaths?
3) How does Shakespeare create tension in Act 5?
4) Does Paris love Juliet? Use examples from Act 5, Scene 3 to support your answer.
5) Do you think Friar Lawrence is presented as a good person? Explain your answer.
6) Write some instructions to a set designer describing how you'd want the inside of the Capulets' tomb to look. Think about the atmosphere you want the set to create.
7) Write your own version of the letter Friar Lawrence says he'll write to Romeo, in Act 5, Scene 2, explaining his plan and all that has happened. Make sure you include all the important information.

Practice Questions

Quick Questions

1) Find a scene where Romeo and Juliet are alone together.
2) Which two characters does Romeo kill?
3) Give two examples of foreshadowing in the play.
4) Give an example of a scene with a lot of humour in it.
5) Pick a line which sums up the character of Tybalt.
6) What is the name of Romeo's servant?
7) Give two examples of imagery that Juliet uses to describe Romeo.
8) Name three characters who use puns in the play.
9) Which two characters are related to the Prince?
10) Find two examples of stage directions.
11) Find part of a scene where the mood is sad.
12) Give three words that describe Mercutio's character.
13) Find an example of a sonnet in the play.
14) Give an example of an oxymoron in the play.
15) Why does Romeo go to Mantua?
16) Find two occasions where Juliet lies to her parents.
17) Give three words which best describe Paris.
18) Find two scenes where a character talks about a dream.
19) Write down two differences between Juliet and Rosaline.
20) Find a scene which contains dramatic irony.

Practice Questions

Theme Questions

1) How does the feud contribute to the tragic outcome of the play?

2) How is Mercutio's attitude towards love different from Romeo's? Explain your answer.

3) How does Juliet's relationship with her family change during the play? Explain your answer.

4) Is Romeo worried about his fate? Find examples to support your answer.

5) How does the mood differ in each of the three fight scenes?

6) How important is religion to the characters in *Romeo and Juliet*?

7) Do you think the older characters in the play have a different view of love than the younger ones? Explain your answer.

8) How does Shakespeare emphasise the role of fate in the play?

9) Why do you think Romeo uses religious imagery to describe Juliet?

10) How does Shakespeare use conflict to increase the tension in the play?

11) Do you think fate plays a role in Romeo and Juliet's first encounter? Explain your answer.

12) Compare the relationships that Romeo and Juliet have with their parents. What are the similarities and the differences?

Character Questions

1) Do you think Romeo is a violent character? Explain your answer.

2) Is Lady Capulet a loving mother? Explain your answer.

3) Why do you think Capulet reacts so angrily when Juliet refuses to marry Paris?

4) Do you think that Mercutio is a good friend to Romeo?

5) Who do you think is more reckless — Romeo or Juliet? Explain your answer.

6) Do you think that Friar Lawrence can be blamed for the tragedy? Explain your answer.

Practice Questions

Character Questions

7) Do you think the Nurse is loyal to Juliet? Explain your answer.

8) Do you think that Juliet is a brave character? Explain your answer.

9) Benvolio and Tybalt react differently to the fighting in Act 1, Scene 1. What does this scene reveal about their characters?

10) Are there any similarities between Romeo and Paris? Give examples to support your answer.

11) What do we learn about Mercutio's character from Act 1, Scene 4 and Act 3, Scene 1?

12) How does Shakespeare show the Prince to be an impressive character?

Technique Questions

1) Why do you think Shakespeare uses foreshadowing in *Romeo and Juliet*?

2) How does Shakespeare use language to show the bond between Romeo and Juliet?

3) *Romeo and Juliet* has a lot of humour in it. What effect does this have on the play?

4) What techniques does Shakespeare use to show grief in the play?

5) What do you think is the significance of light and dark imagery in the play?

6) The events of *Romeo and Juliet* take place over a few days. Why do you think Shakespeare chose such a short period of time for the play?

7) What effect does Romeo and Juliet's bird imagery have on the way you think about them?

8) Do you think that Mercutio's death changes the mood of the play? Explain your answer.

9) Find three examples of dramatic irony. Why do you think Shakespeare uses dramatic irony?

10) Why do you think that Shakespeare uses puns and wordplay in *Romeo and Juliet*?

11) Pick a soliloquy from the play and explain its significance to the plot.

12) Shakespeare includes a wide range of oxymorons (words that contradict each other) in several speeches. Why is this important to the play?

The Characters from 'Romeo and Juliet'

Phew! You should be an expert on *Romeo and Juliet* by now. But if you want a bit of light relief and a quick recap of the play's plot, sit yourself down and read through *Romeo and Juliet — The Cartoon*...

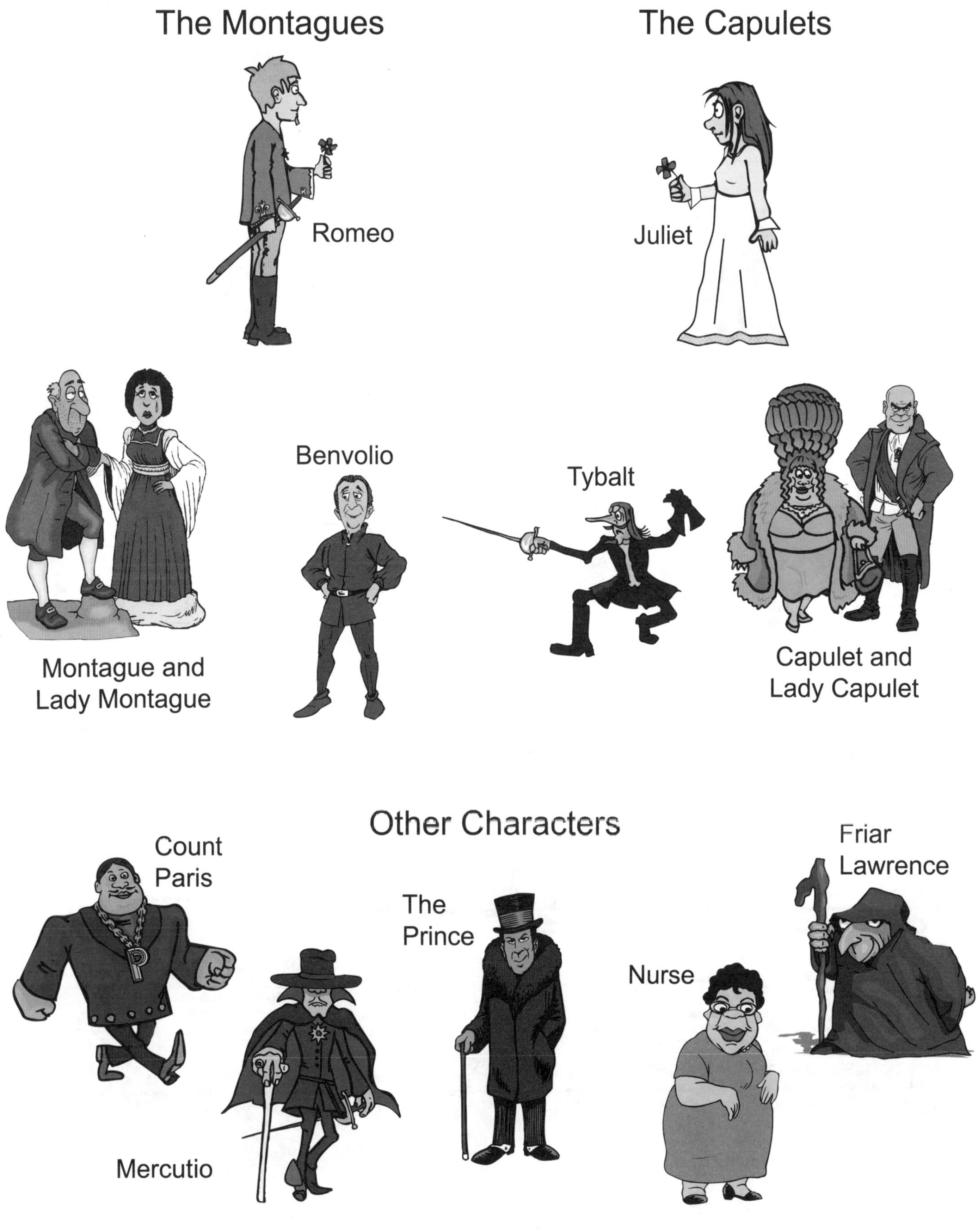

The Montagues

The Capulets

Romeo

Juliet

Montague and
Lady Montague

Benvolio

Tybalt

Capulet and
Lady Capulet

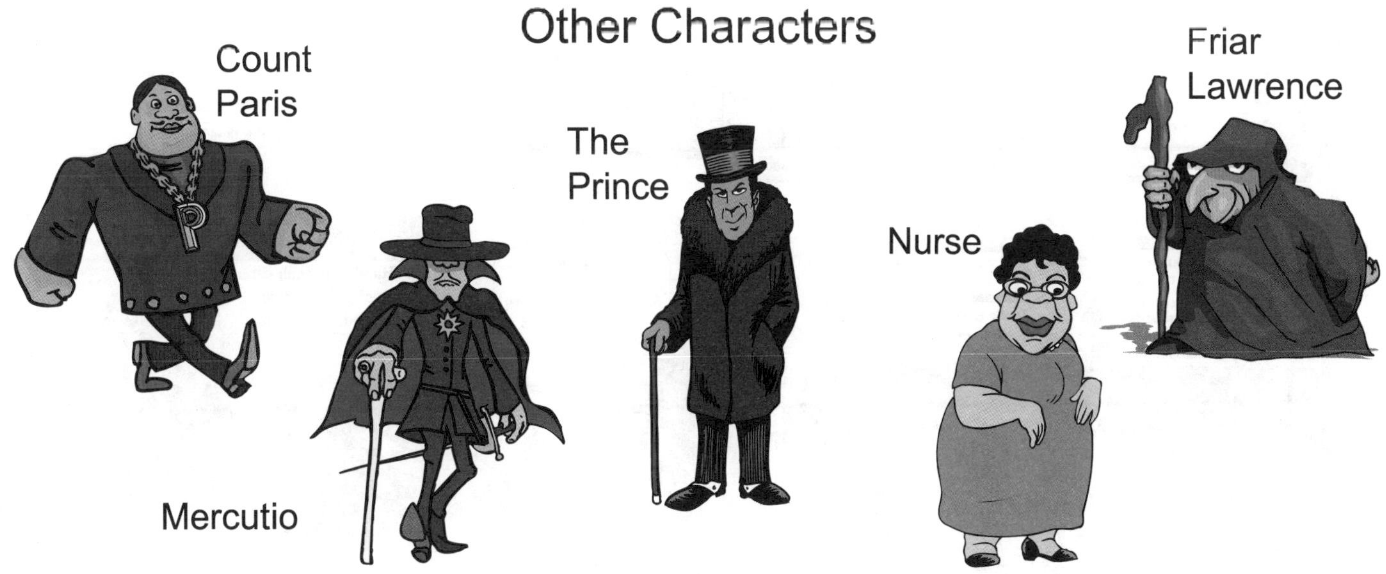

William Shakespeare's 'Romeo and Juliet'

EPR44